1960S PURPLE SEX GAS

SPACE SCRAP 17 BOOK TWO

ERICK DRAKE

SANDS CREATIVE (FTG) PUBLICATIONS

ISBN: 978-1-8383145-3-8

Published by Sands Creative (FTG) Publications

All enquiries to: info@erickdrake.com

Cover Design by James at GoOnWrite.com

Proofreading by Anya Hastwell (twitter @Editorial_Cat)

This book is intended for mature readers only. That is to say, mature readers with an immature sense of humour.

This book is a work of fiction. Names, characters, places, and incidents are products of the author's imagination. Any resemblance to actual persons, living or dead, businesses, events or locales is entirely coincidental.

For Erick Drake books and promotions visit

www.erickdrake.com

For Gemma, Andrew, Clive, Joe and Bronte,

Space Scrap 17 could be read as a metaphor for life (it *could* be read that way but I wouldn't recommend it): stuff happens — some of it big, some of it small, some of it scary. A lot of it 'meh'.

As adults, we are thrust into the midst of it all and left to make what sense of it we can. None of us feel up to the task, all of us feel like fakes, and we often wonder if we can survive. The one thing we do not feel like is 'adult'. So we wait patiently for that magical day when we cease to be children, when we finally complete our transition and become a fully fledged, all powerful, all knowing adult. Because adults understand this stuff and know how to handle it. . .right?

Well, while I wait, still, for that magical transition to happen to me, my advice to you is to adopt this response to life:

Point and laugh.

To date, this is the only response I can find that makes sense.

Oh, and love. Do that, as much of it as you can. With squirty cream and a flake. Pointing and laughing at the world is so much better with loved ones.

And Clive...sorry, which alternative dimension are you from?

CONTENTS

1 /   GIANT SPACE BABIES IN
SPACE

"Huн."

On the bridge of garbage transport Space Scrap 17, second officer Steve Power inclined his head slightly. He checked the sensor readings once more.

"Huh," he grunted again.

Captain Daisy Daryl looked over at the helm station from her place in the captain's chair.

"Something troubling you, Mr Power?"

"There's some weird stuff going on outside the ship."

Daisy sighed and shut down the complex calculations she had been running from her command chair arm displays. It was a relief to turn her attention to something less complicated than ensuring her virtual farm had sufficient livestock to avoid being shut down by a virtual Miasma Inc.

"Mr Power, is that supposed to be an official report?"

"Nope."

"Would you like to make it an official report?"

"There's some weird stuff —"

"That is not an official report."

"OK"

Daisy tapped her finger on the arm of the chair. When no further comment was forthcoming, she tried a pointedly loud 'Ahem.' Still nothing.

"Mr Power, what is happening?"

"I told you."

"Not officially."

"No, not officially, actually. Weird stuff. Outside."

Daisy sighed again. She really needed to work on crew discipline, but she hadn't had time to focus properly on anything since she had taken command. Not with having a vast, alien Doomsday Machine trying to turn them all into a vast, alien Doomsday Machine dinner.

"OK Steve, tell me what's going on."

"Is that a formal command?"

"Second Officer, tell me what is going on outside my ship before I have you shoved into the waste recycling chute."

"Well, in the words of the song 'Giant space babies surround us, baby'."

"In the words of — sorry, what song?"

"The giant space baby song . . . you know, '*I love you / You are my only love / Giant space babies surround us, baby / and also the rich are all bastards*'. That was . . . that was a song wasn't it?"

"No."

"Oh."

"Singing on the bridge is now banned. If that was singing and you aren't in pain?"

He shook his head.

"Right. Well then, singing on the bridge is now banned."

"Aye, aye Captain. Oh," he said, glancing down at his monitors in surprise, "And now our navigation MASERs have opened fire on them."

"What? Why? How? But mostly, why? And how? What?"

Steve's mouth opened and closed a few times as he groped for any words that could better describe what the sensor colonies on the ship's hull were showing him. "I suppose the sensors could just be making shit up again?"

"Making . . . Steve, are you going to talk sense anytime soon?"

"Our sensors are basically vast colonies of specialist bacteria covering the hull. They haven't had an upgrade since the ship was built and they get . . . well, bored. So sometimes, they just make shit up."

"Right."

"Well, that's why no one uses them anymore. They were declared horrifically unstable and withdrawn from the market. Most of them retired and went into politics." He frowned. "Maybe I'm misinterpreting the sensor data. Oh, I know! I'll run a system check with my new face tattoos."

Daisy clenched her teeth. Again with the face tattoos.

He had ordered them online one night after a heavy drinking session with Michigan Jones, the ship's XO. They had all seen the ads;

"Want to be more intelligent? Order our new biotek face tattoos. Don't like the idea? That's because you're stupid. Which you won't be with our new biotek face tattoos! And don't worry about having sentient bio-cultures etched into your face — they'll grow on you. Literally! Order today."

The robo-tattooist arrived the next morning while Steve was sleeping it off, and when he awoke — well, Daisy was pretty sure they could have heard the screams in the next galaxy. He eventually got used to the idea, and now he wouldn't shut up about them. No one had the heart to point out they made him look like a cross between a furious Maori and a manic pagan priest.

"Nope," he said after a moment. "Green lights all the way. According to my face tattoos. On my face."

"Oh good," said Daisy noncommittally.

"Hang on." Steve activated the viewscreen.

"Ah. Well, that's the what," he reported. "As to the why and the how, beats me."

Daisy rose from her command chair slowly. "Whu —?" she pointed at the viewscreen.

Floating in space outside the hull of Space Scrap 17 were several . . . several . . .

"Giant, inert space babies," Steve nodded his approval. "Good."

"Good?"

"Means the sensor colonies are still sane. Trust me, that's good."

"But where did they come from?"

"Us apparently. Ejected from cargo bay four. But that's not the interesting bit."

"It isn't?"

"No. That is." Steve pointed at the screen.

Daisy turned her attention back to the main

viewscreen and watched as the giant space embryos, gently bobbing around within foetal sacks in the silent vacuum of space, exploded as energy weapons tore into them.

"Steve, what's the source of those energy weapons?" Daisy spun on her heel and headed back to the command chair.

"Also us," said Steve.

She halted mid-step. "Computer, why are we shooting space babies? Computer?"

"YES? WHO IS SPEAKING PLEASE?" Daisy winced as the distorted sound of the computer's voice interface bellowed across the bridge.

"Mic, can you do anything with that?"

Mic Vol, communications officer, considered the workable options. Then he considered other, less workable options, including half a dozen metaphysical ones. Yes, that one. He regarded the captain.

"No," he said.

Daisy gave him a flat look. "What about turning down the volume?"

"Ah." Mic rocked back, or rather his triangular encounter suit did. "Might work," he conceded. He stabbed a button. "Volume decreased."

"Computer, you know who I am. You have voice recognition routines — use them."

"I COULD DO THAT, BUT IT WOULD INVOLVE ME RUNNING A REAL-TIME SEARCH AND COMPARE ROUTINE ON MY BINARY WAVE FILES, AND FRANKLY I HAVE WAAAAAAYYYYY TOO MUCH OTHER STUFF GOING ON RIGHT NOW. SO JUST TELL ME WHO YOU ARE."

Daisy and Steve exchanged glances. Steve shrugged.

"Computer has been a bit . . . stressy lately. Not surprising, the operating system is at release 0.01. Never had an upgrade."

"0.01?" Daisy cleared her throat. "0.01?" she repeated, this time in a voice less shrill and embarrassing. "Bloody hell, what level are they on now?"

"7.9.12.6"

"What about the regular upgrades?"

"You don't get regular upgrades with the free beta test version."

"Steve, we need to upgrade."

"We can't afford to upgrade."

Daisy massaged the bridge of her nose between her thumb and index finger.

"Alright. Fine. Computer, this is Captain Daisy Daryl. First, I want to know why we are shooting at giant space babies. Second, I want to know why there are giant space babies. Third, I want to know . . . what are giant space babies?"

"FIRST, WE AREN'T. SECOND, THERE AREN'T. THIRD, SUGGEST SCIENCE STATION REVIEW 20TH CENTURY DOCU-MENTARY 2001: A SPACE ODYSSEY."

"That will explain what they are?"

"WILL IT? GREAT — DO THAT THEN."

"Computer, we can see them. The sensor colonies can see them. We can all see them. Look for big, floaty, exploding things outside the ship and stop shooting them."

"Stop shooting who?"

Daisy froze.

"Is that any way to greet daddy, little Miss Silly Knickers?"

Oh joy.

Daisy turned to the viewscreen, glaring at everybody as she did so. One smirk, just one . . .

"Admiral, to what do we owe this honour?"

"Ah, straight to business. She wasn't always so formal, you know."

"Dad . . ."

"No, she used to run around with her knickers on her head shouting 'look at me, I'm silly knickers'."

A shrill, staccato laugh escaped Daisy's lips. "Ah,

the Admiral's famous sense of . . . bloody . . . humour. Dad, I'm in the middle of something. We need to do this later."

"So I heard. Why are you emitting giant, inert space babies? Have you run out of celebration fireworks? That's my girl, always able to improvise. The mark of an excellent captain."

"Dad, I need the viewscreen. Our operating system is so out of date it contains Trojan horses older than the original Trojan horse and if I want to know what's going on, I have to look out the window. So, can we do this another time?"

"Captain," Steve actually raised his hand.

Daisy turned to Mic and drew her hand across her throat in a slicing motion, the universal sign for cutting communication.

Unfortunately, Mic Vol's race had a completely different universal sign for cutting communication.

So he just stared at her.

Daisy repeated the slicing motion, more urgent this time.

He turned. No, nothing behind him.

He turned back.

Nonplussed, he mirrored the motion back to the captain.

"Jeebuzz, just cut the bloody channel!" Daisy shouted.

"Bit rude," muttered Mic. He pressed 'Mute'.

"Thank you," said Daisy, with all the restraint of a volcano overdue an eruption. "Steve, what is it?"

"Sudden idea. I can cross-link my face tattoos with the computer so it can see the floaty exploding things and stop shooting them."

"Really? Are you sure they can do that?"

He shrugged.

Good enough. "OK, do it. Mic, re-open channel."

The admiral reappeared on the viewer. "About bloody time," he grumbled.

"Admiral, we really need to upgrade the computer. It's on the verge of collapse. You need to authorise the funds for us to buy a full working version of the operating system."

"I have an associate who can get a copy for me."

"No Dad, no under the counter software, no knock offs, rip offs or beta versions. We need a fully working, fully authentic version of ThingStuff 7.9.12.6. I'm sorry, but as captain of this ship, I must insist. I need you to authorise the Pump coins."

Late in the twenty-third century, Earth had amalgamated all its currencies into one: the Pump coin. They considered this crypto-currency to be a foolproof way to control inflation. To increase its value, all they had to do was pump it up by saying how great it was, whereas if they needed to devalue, they'd simply bad-mouth it.

"Well, I'm sorry too Silly Knickers, but you can't have your pocket money just now."

Daisy closed her eyes and took a deep, steadying breath.

Being captain wasn't working out the way she had imagined. Where were the rainbow unicorns and kittens? Where was her indomitable self-confidence? Having an efficient crew and a working computer that was slightly less neurotic than she was would be a big help. Not that she was neurotic. Oh god, was she neurotic?

She headed for the rear of the bridge.

"Mic, I'll take this in my broom cupboard."

"Ready room," said Steve.

"Ready room," she raised her thumbs in a gesture that resembled a flinch.

DAISY STOOD JUST inside the door and waited for it to squeal itself shut.

How long since the damn thing had seen a drop of oil? She would have fired the maintenance manager if they had one. Which they didn't, because they couldn't afford it.

Damn it, she couldn't even fire anyone!

When the fingernails-on-a-chalkboard squeal finally fell silent, she moved over to the desk and opened her private channel.

"Ah, there you are," the admiral grinned at her, his feet on his desk. "How do I look?"

She stifled a laugh.

His new toupee sported an outrageous bouffant. She considered telling him how ridiculous it looked . . . he was her father, after all. But no, she needed

Pump coins for the computer upgrade. Best to keep him sweet. For now.

"It's, um, yes. Yes, it matches your . . . so anyway, Father you look . . . well."

"Father? Daisy, are you calling from the nineteenth century?"

"Well, our chief engineer is a Victorian industrialist."

"What?"

"Oh yes. Forget quantum mechanics, according to Mr Kettlewick, the miracle of steam engineering is the future."

"What the hell are you babbling about, child? Wait, are you in the broom cupboard?"

"It's my ready room. I wanted a ready room. This is my ready room. It *was* the broom cupboard. It is now my ready room. I gave all the brooms to Mr Kettlewick. He marvelled at the technology. Anyway, start again. Hello Dad."

The admiral looked confused for a moment. "We . . . we've already met Daisy. I saw you being born!"

"Yes, I —" Daisy took a slow breath. "What can I do for you, Dad?"

"Ah, well, I have news of your next mission. And although you dumped a vast amount of sewage onto the Ululation homeworld during your last mission, the Yerbootsian government has paid us three times the agreed price."

"Good, because this ship seriously needs some upgrades."

"My thoughts exactly. And once we get paid for the next job, we can get them done."

"For example, we urgently need a — sorry, what? Next job? Why after the next job? The Yerbootsians just paid triple our invoice."

"Oh, you know about that?"

"You just told me."

"Bugger. Well, yes, they did. Unfortunately, I've already spent it."

"What? How? On what?"

He pointed with both hands at his new hairpiece. "It's all the rage."

Daisy blinked at him. "Dad, the only thing holding this ship together is its own gravity. We can't complete another mission with the ship in this state!"

"I'm sorry Silly Knickers, it's just . . ." His eyes grew moist. "I've never actually had that many pump coins before, not even when I sold your sweet, fresh embryonic stem cells."

"You did what?"

"And I was walking past the Harrods designer wig section and they had this little beauty. The money literally went to my head. I am going to be an absolute smash at this month's Wig Club. Peter Fondle will literally be sick. Now we'll see who's president for life. In headwear terms, this is both the dog's bollocks and the bee's knees. Imagine that!"

Daisy tried and failed to imagine that.

"It's . . ." He looked away, as if to avoid the gaze of the camera. He was silent for a moment, eyes blinking rapidly. "It's the wig I've always wanted."

Her throat clenched, abashed by the sight of her father, this giant of a man, her guide and mentor, suddenly vulnerable. "Dad?"

Was that a tear on his cheek?

"Oh hang on, it's leaking again." He swiped at his cheek with a sleeve. "Oh, by the way, the Ululation government has expressed concern that their new prophet will not be staying with them on the Nonsense Sphere. I have agreed for them to send a biographer aboard. So they can document his profound utterances and so on."

Daisy stifled a grin. Michigan Jones would hate that. "He'll love that. I'll tell him the good news personally."

"Good. Now Daisy, I don't think you're going to like this next mission but it's an errand of great mercy." His face grew stern and sombre. "Sometimes people can slip through the system, find themselves beyond the reach of much needed help. Such times, such needs, require heroes to step forward."

"You want me to see if I can find some heroes?"

"No Daisy, you and me and young Michigan Jones are the heroes."

"Wait, what? No, we're not." It had only been a week since their encounter with the Doomsday Machine, and that had almost finished them. They were lucky to have escaped in one piece. Not to mention the minor fact that she was totally unqualified for her position and had not had time to get to grips with her new job. The last thing she needed was a mission fit for heroes.

"Well, you will be after this. A fatal epidemic of Plagues Disease has broken out on a planet called New Amsterdam. New Amsterdam is, how shall I say, a recreation world. A pleasure planet."

"Great. I'll organise shore leave," she said flatly. "Been ages since I had a fatal epidemic. Had a recreational colonoscopy once."

The admiral nodded enthusiastically, "Me too."

"What is . . ." Daisy paused, his last comment sinking in. She shook her head, banishing the associated images. "What is Plagues Disease?"

"Nasty. Laboratory grown. The scientists over at

Miasma were trying to find a health virus. One that promotes health and vitality and could spread just like an ordinary cold."

"And?"

"They created a virus alright, but it cannot distinguish between good and bad microorganisms. It kills all bacteria — including those necessary for a healthy life. Now, there is a cure, but they cannot produce it in sufficient quantities. Not legally, anyway."

"Why?"

"It requires a vital ingredient to act as a catalyst. Bromidium."

"Ah," Daisy nodded. "Bromidium, yes, I see the problem."

"You've heard of it?"

"No."

"Well, it's incredibly useful but bloody difficult to make. The problem is, it's composed of three panacea atoms and one placebo atom. Technically, you can use anything for the placebo atom, you just believe that it *is* a placebo atom and hey presto, it is. But panacea atoms are harder to produce. For those, you need the raw, naked, lubed-up power of an engineered supernova. And a very fine net."

"I don't see how we can help," said Daisy,

"Unless the mission is to heroically stay the hell away from New Amsterdam, in which case sign me up."

"Now, I said they cannot 'legally' produce it in sufficient quantities. However, there is an alternative that is similar enough to Bromidium to enable production of an effective cure. But it has to be distilled from a rare gas."

"Rare gas? What rare gas?"

"It's known as '1960s purple sex gas'. PSG for short."

What new madness was this? "1960s purple sex gas. Right. And just what is 1960s — what is PSG?"

"Ah, well, it's a fascinating story. Back on Earth in the late twentieth century, there were many television entertainment programmes made in a period known as 'the spy boom'. Inevitably, in each episode, the secret agent hero would be knocked out by a gas fed into a locked room through an air vent. To make the gas visible to the viewers, the producers would opt for an industry standard purple vapour."

"Doesn't sound like it would have any medical applications?"

"Not then, no. The manufacturers thought demand would last forever. They produced enormous quantities of the stuff. But eventually people lost interest and the spy-boom went the way of the Western."

"The what?"

"The — oh, never mind. Suffice to say, the demand for purple gas dropped to zero. The manufacturers didn't know what to do with it, and so eventually they just loaded the surplus into metal drums and buried it. And that is where things would have ended, but over the centuries, the gas mutated. It developed a range of unfortunate properties. In small doses, it acts as an extremely powerful aphrodisiac."

"I would have thought that would make it quite popular."

"And in larger doses it causes horrific and unpredictable mutations."

"Instead of acting as an aphrodisiac?"

"*In addition* to acting as an aphrodisiac. The results are something of a nightmare, as you can imagine."

Unfortunately, he was right. Daisy shuddered and stopped imagining. "So why do we have to get involved?"

"Well, as I say, in its raw state, PSG doesn't mix well with . . . well, with anything living. But when distilled correctly, it has the same properties as Bromidium. Which means they can use it as the catalyst required to manufacture the cure for Plagues Disease. In quantity. Unfortunately, PSG is a banned substance across the galaxy. If caught smuggling, sorry, transporting it, the penalty can be either a suspended sentence of community service or death by torture, depending on the judge."

"Forget it."

"Too late, the contracts are signed. There is a quantity of PSG on its way to you as we speak."

"What sort of quantity?"

"Vast."

"No. No chance. Even if I were stupid enough to break the law and risk the lives of my crew, this ship is a disaster just waiting to explode or implode or something else bad ending in 'plode'. There is no way we can undertake a dangerous mission like that with this ship. I wouldn't trust the computer to boil an egg."

The admiral pursed his lips. "Daisy, if we break this contract, then we won't get paid and no one will work with us again. No pumps, no upgrades."

"Forget it Dad, you can't blackmail me."

"No, fair enough. I blame myself. I pushed you too hard. You're clearly not cut out to be captain. It's not your fault. I'll give Michigan Jones a call —"

"Go ahead. You really think I'm that easy to

manipulate, that I'm that insecure, that I'd go to any extreme to prove myself to you or anyone else?"

"Yes."

He had her there. "Right, yes, but . . . well, he'll tell you the same thing. Even he's not that stupid."

"Are you sure?"

She frowned. "No, you're right, he is that stupid. Alright, fine, I'm in. When does it arrive?" she said, instantly hating herself.

"That's my silly knickers. Should be with you in three hours."

"That's Captain, Admiral. Captain Daisy Daryl. If you're asking me to do this, you could at least show me some respect. Now if you'll excuse me, I have three hours to patch up my computer system and prep my crew for certain death."

"Oh, also," the admiral added, "I have arranged for a consignment of smart wigs to be sent to the ship."

"Smart wigs?"

"Three hundred and sixty-five of them. One for each day of the year. My collection will be the envy of Wig Club. Forward to me upon completion of the mission."

"Yeah, sure, no problem," said Daisy airily, feeling anything but 'yeah, sure, no problem'.

The admiral beamed. "Ah, you are so my father's daughter."

"What?"

"Er . . . you are so your father's daughter?"

"You're my father."

"Right! You are so *my* daughter! Or second cousin twice removed. One of those I think. Anyway, bon voyage Captain Daryl."

Daisy finished the call with a sigh and left the broom cupboard.

Why did she always let him talk her into things? She was supposed to be captain and yet no one ever took her seriously. She might as well not be there.

She bit her lip. Had she just screwed up?

To hell with it. Things were going to change. From now on she would stand up for herself and if people didn't like it, well, to hell with — mind you, they might have a point. What if she was making a huge mistake?

No. Wrong mindset, Daisy, she chided herself.

I am Daisy 2.0, the new, determined Daisy. And the new me starts right here, right now. Right after this next mission.

Probably.

Dammit, where the hell was Jones?

DAISY STRODE onto the bridge at a pace, the very picture of brisk efficiency.

"Ah, Captain," Mic said, "Cargo bay master reports we have taken on board a consignment of," Mic inclined his encounter suit's head segment, "'Smart wigs'?"

Daisy nodded, "Thanks Mic. Notify the admiral, would you? We'll have to deliver them after our next mission."

"Very well. Also, our standard resupply requisitions have been delivered. Everything we asked for, but there are a few substitutions. You will need to approve."

Typical. She was such a useless captain they countermanded even her shopping orders. The admiral may have a point after all. She sighed. *Come on, Daisy 2.0, remember?* "Fine, what are the substitutions?"

"We ordered semi-skimmed milk, for which they've substituted a crate of coconuts."

"OK, I suppose that makes sense. Sort of. Anything else?"

"Loaf of medium sliced bread, for which they've substituted . . . a spanner."

"That makes less sense."

"Extra set of kitchen knives for the galley, for which they've substituted a 'slow, bitter relationship breakdown'. A six kilogram packet of cocaine —"

"Who the hell ordered cocaine?"

"No, that was the substitution. They're out of sugar. Instead of yoghurt, we have one hundred and seventeen packets of 'Itch-away Thrush Treatment'. They have substituted soy sauce with a 'coy glance from the delivery driver'. No potatoes, so they've given us apples and instead of apples they've substituted potatoes. And finally, a crate of cock rings instead of — oh, no, sorry, we actually ordered those."

"Who — no, I don't want to know. OK, approved. Anything else?"

"Oh yes. No recycling bags, so they've given us a consignment of 'Lucky Weapons'."

"Lucky weapons? What the hell are lucky weapons?"

"Ooh," piped in Steve, "Didn't think they were still around."

"What are they?"

"You know, things like 'lucky torpedoes' or 'lucky grenades' and the like. No need to aim, you literally just fire and forget because you'll always get lucky and hit the target."

"Never heard of them."

"That's because they were outlawed. By digital marketing agencies."

"Why?"

"Well, they're the only product on the market that doesn't require marketing. By definition, you'll always get lucky and have one when you need it. Marketing agencies couldn't have that, dangerous precedent, cuts them right out of the loop. They had them banned."

"Huh. Right, OK Mic, substitutions approved. Now, Steve, how goes the sensor recalibration?"

"Well, the computer can now see the space babies."

"Great, so it's stopped shooting them?"

Steve shrugged. "It says it wasn't shooting at them in the first place."

"Well, something was, are you sure that — no, never mind, we'll deal with that later. Steve," she lowered her voice, "I have a job for your face tattoos."

Daisy looked around conspiratorially. Steve, uncertain of what was coming, followed suit. She angled herself towards him. Confused, and now slightly alarmed, he angled himself away from her.

"Steve, could you — stop moving away from me! Listen, could you hack the ThingsNStuff omni-site? Specifically, the upgrade section?"

"Er, well yes, I suppose. To do what?"

"I want to upgrade the computer. We've got a vitally important mission coming up and I need it operating at full capacity."

He puffed out his cheeks. "Well, that would be a novel experience."

"But I can't pay for it."

"Captain, I'm a navigation officer, not a thief."

"No, no, no, not thieving Steve. Borrowing. Look, we need the computer to complete our next mission and we need to complete our next mission so that we'll have the pump coins to buy the upgrade. See?"

A slow smile spread across Steve's face. He nodded. "Well, it's been a while. I'll see what I can do."

"Great." Daisy straightened, paused, and looked around again. "Steve, can we do the thing?"

He sighed. Every captain he'd ever met . . .

"Fine."

Daisy beamed. "How long will it take, Second Officer?" she said, loud enough for the rest of the bridge to hear.

"Two hours, Captain," replied Steve, equally loud.

"You've got thirty minutes."

"Oh no," Steve deadpanned, "Well, I'll have to bypass the . . ." Steve looked around then gestured vaguely at something across the room, "That thing over there."

"Excellent. Make it happen, Mr Power." Daisy turned and made to walk away.

"Captain?" Steve's voice stopped her in her tracks.

"Mr Power?"

He looked uncomfortable. "You . . . you know it'll really take a couple of hours, yeah?" he said, sotto voce.

She looked around to make sure no one had overheard, then turned back to Steve, gave a quick nod and marched away, pleased with herself.

Daisy 2.0! How's that for initiative?

She imagined explaining her brilliant command decisions to an interviewer at the Captain of the Year Awards:

"How did I save millions of lives with a neurotic computer and undisciplined crew?" She'd probably add a knowing laugh. *"Initiative. Courage. Innovation. Leadership."* A better quote occurred to her, *"To lead a ship, you need leader-ship." Interviewer looks impressed, audience claps spontaneously. She smiles and nods modestly.*

Now to break the news to Michigan Jones. Somehow, she didn't expect spontaneous applause from him.

Spontaneous combustion was way more likely.

Ancient Soviet Russia was once a country famous for its show trials, paranoia, ruthless secret police and so many weapons of mass destruction that they could destroy the world several times over.

Doctor Smiert sighed.

You just didn't get that level of thoroughness today. If only she had been born back then. The Russia of today? She snorted. It reminded her of something her great-grandmother used to say: *"Full bellies don't plough fields."* By all the Aspirational Concepts, she missed that woman.

The medical station chimed, interrupting her thoughts. Smiert's excited fingers danced across the controls with practised ease. Her face dropped. Another failure.

She had followed the same cycle all day; excited

experimentation, crushing failure, then frustrated anger. Well, at least she got to shoot something.

She rubbed her hands down her lab coat to make sure they were dry, and once more put her eye to the optical viewfinder.

"Computer," she said through gritted teeth, "Eject accelerated growth experiment twenty-seven."

She watched through the targeting system as the giant amniotic sac bobbed and bounced into the vacuum of space.

Sweat formed around Smiert's eye as she pressed it against the rubber eye guard of the MASER targeting scope.

As she had done many, too many, times before that day, she steadied her breathing and traced the trajectory of the ejected inert biological tissue, moving the cross hairs not at the sac itself, but at a point ahead of its current position. The words of her old tutor at Miasma's Ministry of Love returned to her: *When targeting a moving object, always shoot where you calculate the target will be, not where it is now.*

That was all very well, but he didn't have to calculate the trajectory of a target that could change direction at any time because of the competing gravitational vectors of Space Scrap 17 and the planet they were orbiting.

She relaxed her finger on the trigger. She could have had the computer do this, but not only had her patch to replicate and speed grow the biomass already overstretched it but also she had programmed it to ignore anything that looked like a giant space baby. Besides, she enjoyed the experience of tracking a target and squeezing the trigger.

She imagined she was a sniper in the old KGB, tracking an enemy dissident and putting a bullet in her head. It made her feel like a little girl again. She steadied her breath and squeezed the trigger.

Space Scrap 17 had nine chromium MASER navigation cannons, each arranged into arrays of three on the front section of the hull: three facing forward, three to port, and three starboard. The port side cannon now flared into life as a MASER pulse tore through space, disintegrating its target.

Direct hit!

Good. Smiert's satisfied smile froze as she felt a cold circle of metal press into the back of her neck. Her combat implants powered up, preparing her for battle.

"Stay perfectly still or I will shoot."

"Jeebuzz!" Smiert shouted. The voice had been

quiet, she knew, but the bio-tek implants amplified her hearing, making the soft voice next to her ear sound like a point blank blast from an air-klaxon.

"Fuck!" she added, in case her original comment had not sufficiently made its point.

Her implants readied data on the location of the vital organs and vulnerable nerve clusters of over four thousand species. As soon as her ocular resolution implants confirmed the identity of the threat, the relevant kill information would load into her combat programs. But she already knew the species of her would-be assailant.

"I really don't think you want to be that close, do you Ambassador Tongue? If nothing else, your perfume will kill me." This was regrettably true. Her enhanced combat aural sensors were also now on high alert and Tongue's cologne felt like a corrosive on the back of her throat. However, that was not the real reason for her comment.

Tongue moved back a few inches.

Hah! Amateur! That was all her combat programs needed.

She hooked her foot around the back of Tongue's leg and rammed her elbow back to where the tactical programs told her his sternum would be.

She heard a satisfying grunt and whipped round,

her back fist outstretched. With a sound like a cross between a slap and a thud, Smiert's knuckles connected hard with Tongue's cheek.

He staggered back, tripping over his own ankle booted feet, and crashed to the floor.

It was then that things stopped going Smiert's way. In fact, things not only stopped going her way, but they made a point of shunning her, added unnecessarily crude, mocking hand gestures and skipped off in a totally different direction altogether.

Bugger.

Tongue sprang into a crouch, death quills instinctively sprouting from his fists as he prepared for battle.

Smiert knew she was dead meat.

But instead of launching into the expected attack, he cleared his throat. The death quills, which made his balled fists look like alarmed hedge-hogs, flattened and receded once more beneath his flesh.

"Smiert, why — no, first things first. *What* are you doing?"

This was an excellent question.

"I am supposed to be destroying you with a devastating mix of expert martial artistry and super-human speed. Instead, I believe what I am doing is best described as . . . dad dancing."

"Oh, you are cognisant of that, good, and now the why?"

Smiert knew exactly why. The status icons on her smart cataracts left her in no doubt.

Once activated, her threat response combat program had taken over her voluntary motor functions, its deadly tactical programs and her enhanced senses controlling her every move.

But the combat program had become scrambled. And, worrying as it was that she was now a helpless passenger in her own body, uncontrollably jerking around like a drunken puppet on a hot tin roof, the cause of her spasmodic jerking was a greater concern. But the last thing she wanted was for Tongue to discover it.

No, she decided. She would bluff it out. "I am elevated on illegal yet freely available narcotics. Is casual, yes? Or maybe I jerk you off?"

Tongue raised a sardonic eyebrow. "Sorry?"

"No, I mean jerk around. Maybe I am jerking around. Not jerk you off. Ha ha, yes, perhaps I am just kidding you, yes? Or maybe what I'm doing is exercise routine to limber up before I eviscerate you?"

"Or maybe you're just talking bollocks," Tongue raised himself from the floor, smoothing the creases from his pretty, form hugging, summer dress. "I've seen the effects of a spasmodic negative cascade in combat implants before. But that can only happen if the programs don't have enough memory to work with. Ah," he snapped his fingers. "Your little patch has overstretched the computer, forcing it to grab additional memory from wherever it can. Oh well, that's karma I suppose."

Smiert frowned. Dammit, he had guessed. And he knew about her patch.

Her system patch was not large by the conventions of the day. But this ship's computer was essentially a relic from the Cambrian explosion, so her patch may as well have been the entire New Vatican library. Now the computer was panicking, grabbing any available memory space from wherever it could find it: DEVICEs, calculators, smart food dispensers . . . and her own combat implants.

"So why are you here, Ambassador?" Smiert had intended her question to be accusatory, but that tone was difficult to achieve now that her body had decided to perform an avant-garde version of a Bolivian leather shorts dance. By all the Aspirational Concepts (Orthodox Eastern Block Region, of course), this computer glitch was making things difficult. Buggeringly difficult.

"Smiert, you've not only crippled the computer with your nasty little program, but you've also helped yourself to large amounts of the ship's pseudo carbon blocks. What's going on?" Tongue frowned. "For the love of flaps, what are you doing now?"

"Twerking, apparently."

"Alright look, this is way too distracting. Not to mention disgusting. I'll help you get control of your implants, and in return, you tell me what you're up to. Deal?"

Much as she wanted to stop jerking and gyrating around the room, Smiert could not, would not, reveal her secrets. Her masters took a very dim view of betrayal. "No deal."

Tongue placed his hands on his perfect, curvaceous hips. "Fine. I'll leave you to your twerking and go ask the captain if she is aware her doctor is fitted with military grade tek. Expensive military grade tek."

Smiert quickly considered her options. She could do this quickly because the number of options she had were precisely zero.

"Alright. Deal. But not here, somewhere more private. Now, override the memory requisition."

Tongue tilted his gorgeous head to the side and gorgeously chewed his gorgeous lip. Gorgeous was the only way Yerbootsian males could do anything. Bastards.

"Right." He moved to a computer interface. Without warning, Smiert regained control of her limbs. She had no time to steady herself and so collapsed to the floor like a string puppet whose depressed puppeteer has just realised he's wasted his life.

"I have the command codes for your implants now," said Tongue, raising his thumb. Damn it, he had a thumb drive! "Especially the dad dancing routine. I'm sure I could write some fun versions myself. Don't let it come to that. In the meantime, stop whatever you are doing with the computer. I look forward to hearing from you. Soon."

Tongue spun on his gorgeous ankle booted heel and gorgeously exited the room, his curvaceous hips swaying gorgeously.

Smiert remained on the floor breathing heavily and glared after the Yerbootsian, imagining the multitude of gorgeous ways she could kill him.

"Now, branding. Would you say you are an utterer or a proclaimer?"

"What?"

"Try saying something profound. Unless you're one of those who just mutter and gnashes their teeth, we could pull that off I suppose?"

Jones couldn't decide what was making him more angry: having his private quarters invaded, being expected to do things, or the nickering modulation of her voice. If it was the latter, he was likely to be angry for some time. WindyMane was, after all, an Ululation. A Zebroid. A humanoid zebra.

"Go on great one, have a mutter and a gnash. Everyone loves a good gnashing, especially if there's lots of muttering. And spittle. Can you manage spittle? Go on, enjoy it, have fun with it."

"I will not gnash or mutter. I can do spittle. Yes, put me down for spittle. No, wait, that's stupid. How about getting drunk? I can do that. Or, better still, I can do getting drunk *and* you can go away."

"Are you sure you're the Great Prophet?"

Was that a disapproving look on her stripy Zebroid face? Somehow, despite his aversion to zebras, Jones had become a mythological prophet to an entire race of them. All he'd done was punch one of them in the face. Well, three of them. All diplomatic delegates to the Loose Association of Sentient Species. And even though at the time he had the excuse of being under the influence of misprescribed stims, this event had somehow not resulted in disaster and a lifetime restraining order. No, of course it hadn't. Apparently, he was now divine. And not in a good way. And now, because of his surprise ascendance to divinity, this . . . whatever she was, had shoehorned herself into his life in the expectation that he would actually do things. And not just any old things, oh no. Things of import.

At first he hadn't minded being declared the Herald of the Second Coming of the mythical Gavin Starmane. After all, he reasoned, once they had effected repairs on Space Scrap 17, he would be on his way, leaving the fawning Ululations far behind.

But they'd conspired to keep their hooves in him. Bloody zebras. He knew they were no good.

"Prophet? No. Yes. Look, it's complicated OK. Why am I explaining myself to you? Go away."

"I cannot go away, see," she held out her lanyard, which contained a photograph of a laughing zebra's head with tidy mane braids, her name and some scrawling text. Jones squinted at it.

"Yes, well, I can't read zebraic. For all I know, that could be an advert for your lanyard printing business."

WindyMane inclined her head slightly and made a "huh" sound. "You are not quite as I expected. This identifies me as your official Poo-Pi-Doo."

"My what?"

WindyMane gently knocked her upper hooves together. "There is no direct translation. A Poo-Pi-Doo . . . it's a kind of cross between official biographer, historian, PR consultant and general spin doctor. I had thought you would be more . . . inspiring, give me some sort of raw material to work with. Bit disappointing. Love a challenge though."

Jones opened the fridge and took out a bottle of Big Papa's Golden Papa Secretions. He saluted her with the small, clear bottle. "You're fired. There.

That's twice I've 'disappointed' you in the space of two sentences."

"Yes, that was almost interesting."

"Thanks. Look, one day I hope to meet someone with whom I want to share my every waking moment. No offence, but that day is not today and you are the wrong species. And I was lying. I don't want to share anything with anyone. Although I dig your mane braids, very fetching."

"Do you intend to produce offspring?"

"Excuse me?"

"That reminds me, I'll need a sperm sample."

"Well, that's very kind of you, but as I say, you're not my species."

"So we can preserve it in case we need to clone you in the future. So you can save us again."

WindyMane held out a specimen pod with an air of expectation. She was doing that annoying head tilt thing again. "I need you to fill this. I'll leave it here," she said, in a Zebroid version of 'prim', before placing the pod on the table between them. The words 'Insta-freeze sperm'o'glug' announced themselves in gaudy lettering on the side.

"Oh come on, I'm good but even I can't hit it from here."

"And is that what you would call humour?" she

clapped her hooves together, and the ghost reappeared, hovering behind her, his quill poised, head leaning forward attentively.

Jones swallowed hard. That was still weird. The apparition had first appeared just after Windy-Mane's unwelcome arrival in his cabin. After Jones had finally stopped screaming, WindyMane explained the Ululations had long ago mastered psychics, the paranormal branch of physics. Through the application of psychics, she explained, the dead enjoyed useful careers as personal assistants and such like. In Jones's honour, she had chosen a human spirit, that of Plato. Whoever the hell he was.

"Jeebuzz. Look, are you sure I can't get you a drink?"

WindyMane opened her muzzle, but a chime interrupted her response.

"Doorbell," said Jones, in response to Windy-Mane's quizzical look. "Come in," he called. As an afterthought he added, "Unless it's work, in which case this is a recorded message. The Michigan Jones you are looking for is unavailable. Please go away and bother someone else."

The door opened.

"Oh. Sorry, I didn't know you had company," said Daisy.

#

Tongue and Smiert sat in miss-matched utilitarian chairs, facing each other in the cramped confines of a storeroom, surrounded by atmosphere suits and various odd-shaped engineering components. The room was in darkness save for a single, small light illuminating the doctor's face.

"My great-grandmother was a very wise woman," Smiert's voice was low and even. "'*Full bellies don't plough fields*,' she used to say. Then she would spit on the dog. I ask her one day, '*Great-grand-mama, why do you spit on your dog?*' and she would shrug and say, '*Is not my dog.*' Then she would spit on me. I ask her one day, '*Great-grand-mama, why do you spit on your great-granddaughter?*' and she would shrug and say, '*You are adopted.*' You have question, Mr Tongue?"

"Two actually." He grimaced and adjusted his bra strap. He hated breaking in new brassieres. "First, why are we sitting in the dark? Put the bloody lights on."

Smiert shrugged. "Bit of atmosphere never hurt." She reached behind her for the light switch.

Tongue winced as the room blazed into harsh, soulless light.

The doctor switched off her torch. "Second question?"

"Why are you telling me about your great-grandmother?"

"Is fitting you know something about the woman who is going to kill you," she shrugged. "Manners cost nothing. Is a courtesy."

"Your great-grandmother is going to kill me?"

"No. She is dead. I kill her."

"Wow. So the news of your adoption didn't go down too well?"

"She was *skankovich* bitch. Anyway, I kill her. I kill you. "

Tongue sighed. Smiert seemed determined to make this difficult. Oh well, he would have to be direct.

"Spongiform Jelloid life forms," he said, amused to see what the reaction would be. He was not disappointed.

"Spongiform Jelloid life forms? Spongiform Jelloid life forms?" Smiert laughed, a strained 'ha ha'. "What is this Spongiform Jelloid life form? This is Yerbootsian humour, yes? Ha ha."

Tongue smiled, a short, tense smile that vanished as quickly as it appeared. "Alright then, and do try to keep up. I know you conduct illegal and unethical experiments where you dabble with creating new life forms. Specifically, for some bizarre, twisted reason of your own," Tongue leant forward, elbows on his knees. It gratified him to note, given the brief flicker of Smiert's eyes, that his new bra was doing its advertised job. Very uplifting. "Specifically, Spongiform. Jelloid. Life forms." He sat back and smiled. "Yes, Smiert, I know of your 'work'. By any civilised measure, you are a sick bastard. Which means you are uniquely qualified to attempt the job for which our employers hired you. Unique as in 'the only one in the galaxy'. Now, in case you missed it, the important words in all that were 'our employers'. I'm your new handler."

"No."

"Yes."

"You?"

"Yup."

A slow smile spread across the doctor's face. "You know what happened to my last handler?"

"No. No one does. She disappeared mysteriously. Last seen on her way to your office for a routine medical checkup."

"She did not survive. Arrive. She did not arrive."

"Huh. That's a nice tattoo on your forearm," Tongue nodded at Smiert's arm. Almost instinctively, she flinched and folded her arms, hiding the image. Hah. "Your last handler, Agent Lethal, had a tattoo just like that. The interesting thing about her is that she was a level 7 Chromatic Aberration. See, that's how important your work is to our employers. They assigned you a handler that a human-rhinoceros hybrid with fists made of razors couldn't take down. And yet," Tongue spread his hands, "you managed it."

"A tattoo you say?" Smiert's expression was all innocence. "Such a coincidence."

"Yes. Except there's no mention of a tattoo in your records."

"Is new."

"Is it. Tell you what," Tongue leant forward again, "Why don't we go to the infirmary and scan your arms? I'm willing to bet your right forearm has slightly different proportions to your left. Not so as you'd notice. But still."

Smiert cocked an eyebrow. "Have you booked your check up yet?"

"Not yet." He held Smiert's eyes for a moment. Then he sat back. "No time. I've been too busy trying to determine why our mission specialist has ignored instructions to conduct her mission discreetly and has instead alerted half the galaxy to the fact that she is creating giant space embryos."

Smiert snorted, "You exaggerate."

"Steve noticed."

"I shall kill him."

"Much as I admire your enthusiasm, Doctor," said Tongue after a momentary pause, "I think the definition of the word 'discreet' may have changed since you last checked."

Smiert threw her hands in the air. "They are running maintenance, is only time computer is even slightly relaxed and I can run patch undetected. What am I supposed to do? This ship has technical resources of an eyebrow."

"Yes, as you say in your reports. Constantly. So you'll be pleased to hear that the problem is in hand. Our employers intercepted the payment transaction my government made to Admiral Daryl. They injected three times the invoice amount into the pay stream. Space Scrap has more than enough to upgrade its computer system. In the meantime . . . the other donor has arrived."

"Ah. Good. And she has met Jones?"

"Yes. Her name's WindyMane."

"Are they copulating?"

Tongue frowned. "They've only just met."

Smiert snorted. "Which century are you from, *sumooshka?*"

"First, '*sumooshka*' isn't a word, even in the Galactix language. Second, and more importantly, they are different species."

"Yes. Good point. They will need to be very drunk."

"Yeah," Tongue shuddered, trying and failing not to think about that. "But our employers consider all scenarios. I will soon have certain narcotics that will . . . sufficiently lower the inhibitions." He shuddered again. Gods, the 'morning after' regrets were going to register on the Richter scale. Better put Human Resources on alert. And an army of psychiatrists.

Smiert's features tightened. "Narcotics? So, you wish to drug me because I will not make love with you."

"What?"

"What?"

Tongue shook his head. He was suddenly impatient to be away from this so-called doctor. "Cargo freighter Non-Stop Exotic Matter will shortly deliver the narcotics. Escorted by a complement of Total Bastards, no less. Like I say, our employers leave nothing to chance. Leave the next phase of the operation to me. You just lie low and pretend to be whatever passes for 'Smiert normal'. And shut down that bloody program. Wait until the computer gets upgraded before you patch it into the core again. Got that?"

"Yes."

"Good girl," Tongue stood to leave.

"I will kill you. One day soon."

Tongue paused at the door. "Maybe. For now, just keep your mind on your job, Doctor."

He left the storeroom.

The encounter had gone about as well as could be expected. He had stalled her. Now all he had to do was prevent Smiert from accomplishing her mission while somehow not revealing he was actually working for the opposition.

Preferably, in a more comfortable bra.

"Do you mind, whoever you are, I am trying to rouse my master."

"Really? I never had any problems." Daisy hated the words even as she said them. But by now her snark was a reflex, a force of habit. She and Jones had been sparring for so long the Broca area of her frontal lobe was just phoning it in.

"WindyMane, this is Daisy Daryl. She's the captain. Captain, this is WindyMane. She's annoying."

"Oh yes," said Daisy, "Your groupie. Dad mentioned something about that."

WindyMane's ears twitched forward. "Oh, you're *the* Daisy Daryl!"

Yes, Daisy thought, yes I bloody well am. "I am she."

WindyMane took a step forward. "The ex, Daisy Daryl the ex, yes, you will have much information. I will interview you."

Daisy screamed.

WindyMane's advance came to an abrupt halt, her features frozen. "What did you just do with your face?" she finally gasped.

Jones shrugged. "She hates being referred to as 'the ex'. It's understandable. She's still not over me. Daisy let it go. If you love me, set me free."

Daisy backed up. "Shut up Jones. I screamed because a ghost just appeared out of nowhere and came at me brandishing a quill, not because some stripy bitch referred to me as 'the ex'! Which, by the way, is factually incorrect." She tore her eyes from Plato's ghost. "I don't wish to split hairs, but he's my ex."

"Oh yeah, the ghost thing. Took me a while to get used to it. It's her PA. Plato, this is the captain. My ex."

Son of a — Daisy wasn't sure if her fists had clenched because she wanted to stop herself punching Jones in his stupid face or because she wanted to punch Jones in his stupid face. Right, well, if that's how he wanted it . . .

"So, WindyMane, you want information about The Mighty Twat here?"

"Hang on," Jones stepped between her and WindyMane, finger raised in the air on a point of order. "When we met, you agreed to full non-disclosure about our relationship."

"No I didn't. Although, I have to say Windy-Mane, there isn't much to talk about. In the sack, he's about as exciting as an actual sack."

"Don't be writing that down!" Jones waved urgently at the spectre.

Plato paused in his scribbling. Eyes fixed on Jones, he slowly lifted the nib of the quill to his mouth, extruded his tongue, and licked at it. The nib made an annoying rasp as it slowly traversed the ancient papillae of his tongue, an organ made arid by a passage of time so stupidly vast it could only be measured in cobwebs. Then he dipped the nib in a spectral inkwell and returned to the *scratch, scratch, scratch* of his writing. The look of hoary contempt never once left his face.

"WindyMane," Jones whirled on the Ululation, "get rid of that ghost, exorcise it, expel it, I don't care — just get rid of it."

"How can I write your biography if I banish him?"

"So he's your ghost writer?" If there were an award for keeping a straight face, Daisy decided, she had just won it.

"Plato only records my notes. I write them up," said WindyMane.

The primness of WindyMane's tone did not escape Daisy. Oh gods, she really made this irresistible. "A platonic relationship then?"

"Daisy, stop taking the piss." Jones took a long gulp of his drink. He held up the bottle. "Ah, Big Papa's Golden Papa Secretions. That's a man's refreshment right there. Wait — why are you here? My shift doesn't start for another two hours, shouldn't you be off somewhere doing captain stuff?"

Daisy sighed. And just when she was beginning to enjoy herself. She straightened her posture and clasped her hands behind her back. How's that for captain stuff? "XO, we need to talk. A . . . mission briefing."

"Talk? No." Jones wagged his finger at her, his face suddenly taut with alarm. "No, I've seen that face before. You're doing that serious face thing. Serious faceage is happening. This is a 'Thing', isn't it. Oh great," he turned to his unwanted groupie. "WindyMane, fetch my deerstalker and pipe — I am about to be assailed by logic traps and ancient

Tibetan memory realignment techniques. Not to mention intense gaslighting. I shall need all my deductive capabilities to hand. Oh, and some opium. No, forget the deerstalker and pipe. Fetch my opium!" Jones spun on his heel and stomped into his bedroom, calling over his shoulder: "Watson, the needle!"

And we're off, thought Daisy. Back when they were a couple and she had wanted to talk, to plan out the future, his first recourse had always been one of ludicrous overreaction. Anything to distract from the point. Because he had no reply to the point. And even if he did, it would no longer be the point but the . . . blunt. And then there would be no point. Daisy stopped herself. Damn it, he'd distracted her again! She opened her mouth to reply, but WindyMane broke in.

"Why do you make someone stalk deer for you?" the puzzled Ululation shouted at the bedroom.

"Deerstalker," came the flat reply. "It's a hat, not a wildlife worrier. Anyway, who said I stalk deer? Have you been talking to the deer? Can't believe HR upheld their complaint. Bastards."

"Anyway," cut in Daisy, "mission briefing."

"Sticking to the point, eh? Take care Windy-

Mane, by my thighs she's a feisty one this new captain."

"Are you getting this, Plato?" The spectre nodded eagerly, his dry chuckle echoing coldly at the back of everybody's skull.

"Is that dead bastard laughing again?" Jones's plaintive cry came from the bedroom. "Windy, tell him to stop, or you can sod off back to the planet."

"Jones, I'm not having a mission briefing shouting at you and," she cut off Jones's instinctive response, "I'm not coming into your bedroom. Come out here. That's an order. You know, captain stuff."

"Mission briefing? You mean the mission briefing you'll give me at the mission briefing meeting? The specific meeting we have where we discuss missions and rigorously assess our briefs?"

Daisy clenched her teeth. "Yes."

"Great. See you at the mission briefing. Door." The door slid open half an inch and then stopped. The mechanism squeaked and then slid closed again.

"What is it with these bloody doors?" muttered Jones, emerging from the bedroom.

"Trust me," she said, "It's impossible to make a dramatic exit on this ship. Look, you're right. I do want a private word. As captain, I'm establishing some new rules. Starting with this mission, we are going to maintain a professional distance. I am Captain, you are Executive Officer. We will interact fully and freely on professional matters. Outside of that, we are strangers. I need to maintain a detached distance."

"Is that it?" said Jones. "Oh, well, that wasn't too painful. Right, well, see you at the mission briefing." Jones indicated to the door.

Daisy shifted awkwardly. "And, uh, as XO I require you to consult with your captain. You know, analyse situations and provide options for consideration. XO stuff."

Jones's face dropped. "Oh no. It's one of those, isn't it? Analysis and options, my arse. You think," he wagged his finger at her, "You think you've made a massive screw up and you want to make me listen while you talk yourself into ever-decreasing circles of doubt and self-loathing. And then, if I say anything other than '*uh-huh*' or '*they must be really jealous of you*', and I offer anything that sounds even remotely like a solution, even if only to shut you the fuck up, then you'll accuse me of '*mansplaining*'."

"See, this is what I'm talking about — I want our exchanges to be on a professional level and while I don't mind a frank exchange of views in private, what you are doing can only be described as personally offensive."

"Don't you dare bring Frank into this. It just happened alright, we were drunk . . . you weren't there for me!"

"That's not the point, I — who the hell is Frank?"

"I have no idea."

Argh! He did it again! Daisy put her hands on her hips. "Right, WindyMane, piss off. This is confidential command stuff. The captain and XO are having a conference."

WindyMane stiffened, gave a huffing snort and left the room, the ethereal remains of Plato bobbing along after her. Once the door had finally squealed itself open and then screamed shut again, Daisy and Jones regarded one another other in silence.

"Now, Jones . . ."

"Ah flaps, you're actually making me do this. OK, fine, but I wasn't joking about that opium — please tell me I have time for some opium?" he groaned, shoulders slumping.

"Michigan, I need to talk to *someone*. You know me. Believe it or not . . . you are the only person on board whose opinion I trust."

A look of remorse crossed Jones's face. He ruffled his unkempt mass of hair. "Oh. Well that's . . . I mean, I didn't think we'd . . . well that's . . . nice? I suppose?"

"Well, I don't know anyone else aboard, so . . ."

He gave her a flat look. "Oh great, cheers."

"You know what I mean."

"Forget it, whatever it is, I don't want to know; the door is over there."

"Right." She'd hoped it wouldn't come to this, but their prior relationship had armed her with a degree of foresight.

She pulled out a tranquilliser gun and shot him.

"Ow! What the bloody hell?!"

"Ululation venom."

"Wait, what? They have venom?!"

"Sub-dermal parasites, to be precise."

Jones's mouth dropped open. "You . . . I've got . . . with . . . did you just say you shot me with sub-dermal parasites?"

"I *think* it said sub-dermal. Maybe it was sub-normal? Anyway, it's a parasite they carry. Harmless to them, it completes its life cycle when an Ululation undergoes something they call 'The Shedding'. Have you heard of that? Once a year, when a female is in heat —"

"You sick bitch!"

"That's *Captain* sick bitch to you. Jones, I need advice and you're the only one who can help me."

"No! Absolutely not! I don't have to listen to this, *Captain*. We're not in a relationship, we're not even friends with benefits. What you want is Talk Buddies. I'm not your lady whisperer. Good day, madam." Jones turned to leave.

"You realise this is your cabin?"

"Yes."

"OK."

He turned back to her, "Even so, I can't leave until I know the answer to one very important question."

"What question?"

"Why don't my legs work?"

"Oh," Daisy beamed. The tranquilliser worked! Yay! "That'll be the parasites. Oh, now, what was it the doctor said . . . ah yes. I am legally obliged to inform you that should you choose to take it, side effects include erectile dysfunction for up to seven days. And paralysis of your arms and legs for around six hours. It means you'll have to do a four-hour shift with no limbs, but that shouldn't affect your usual work rate."

"At what point did I agree to you shooting me with parasites, you maniac?"

"Ah, no, I'm not legally obliged to give you a choice. Only to tell you what the side effects are. Captain stuff. Anyway, look, sit down while the parasites secrete their immobilisation protein."

"What? Why do they need me immobile?"

"So their eggs can hatch safely. Jones?"

Jones swayed and then collapsed backward onto his battered old sofa.

"Oh, and you'll produce excessive saliva. Something about your taste cells mistaking the secretions for citrus. Like biting into a lemon. Oh, lemon venom, that's funny."

"No ish gucking fishnet," Jones spat through the seeming ocean of saliva that now gushed uncontrollably down his chin.

"So anyway, now I have your undivided attention. Jones, I think I've made a huge screw-up."

Jones released a forlorn moan.

DAISY WHEELED Jones into cargo bay seven.

She had spent the last hour and a half telling him all about her accepting their latest mission and how she felt pressured by her father and her frustrations with the state of the ship. She had intended to leave it at that, but once she started talking, she confessed all her doubts and fears; including the fine details of her conflicting thoughts about whether or not she was cut out for the job.

Did the crew like her? She thought they did, but . . . well, could she be sure they did? What if they didn't?

She felt much better after unburdening herself.

It was so nice to have someone willing to just sit there and listen for once. Well, not so much 'willing to listen' exactly, more 'incapable of leaving'. Whatever.

It worked. She had only stopped when the intercom chimed and the cargo bay informed her of the PSG's arrival. Daisy ordered up a wheelchair, bundled the now glazed-eyed Jones into it and left for the cargo bay.

Upon arrival, Kerim, the bay master, immediately confronted her.

"Captain. You know anything about smart wigs?"

"Yes, of course I know about the smart wigs. I'm the captain."

"Good, just arrived, sign here."

Tongue sashayed into the bay. Daisy vaguely wondered why he was there. Cargo shipments were not within his bailiwick as science officer. "Good morning, Captain. Everything under control?"

Daisy bristled. "Yes, Science Officer, everything is under control. Why wouldn't it be under control?" Daisy resented the implication things might not be under control. The implication resented her resenting it. It was, after all, just doing its job.

Tongue directed a pointed look at Michigan Jones, slouched and dribbling in the wheelchair. "Drunk already?"

"Har bloody har," said Jones through an ocean of spittle. "Shouldn't you be at the hairdressers?"

Tongue's hand instinctively reached for his hair before he caught himself and lowered it again. He shot Jones a sarcastic look and turned to Daisy.

"Captain, this consignment of PSG, I'll need to check the safety seals are in place."

"They're not," said Kerim.

"What? Well, where are they?" put in Daisy.

"On a break. It's fish day in the canteen."

Daisy put her hands on her hips. "Well, get them back in here; this consignment is hazardous. One crack in those containers and we could end up with orgies and explosions."

"And not in a good way," added Jones.

"Union rules state that the safety seals get to eat their body weight in fish after they've stowed each consignment. They've just finished stowing the smart wigs. Do you want to risk a walk-out by the seals?"

"Undulation," said Tongue.

"What?"

"Technically, seals don't walk. They undulate."

Kerim looked blank. "What?" he said again.

"They extend their head and shoulders forward and then draw their pelvis up. Like a caterpillar."

"Yes, thank you, Science Officer," Daisy cut in,

"Whatever they do, we need to ensure the PSG containers are —"

"Great one!" WindyMane nickered as she skip-walked into the bay, followed by another two Ululations.

"Oh bloody hell," this was all Daisy needed. "XO kindly tell your zebra groupie and her groupie groupies to bugger off."

Jones twisted in his wheelchair. "Zebra groupie and zebra groupie groupies, kindly bugger off. Captain's orders."

WindyMane came to a halt before Jones. "I have Balms and Unguents!"

"Sounds painful," said Jones.

"Hello," said Balms.

"Hello," said Unguents.

"They are highly regarded doctors from my homeworld. I have asked them to treat you."

"Treat me? What, you mean with cake and binge drinks? Fantastic, I'm having a shit day."

Balms, Unguents and WindyMane exchanged a look and then made an odd nickering sound.

"What are they doing?" asked Tongue.

"I think it's what passes for an Ululation laugh," said Jones.

"No, Awesome One, not cake," said Windy-Mane, "they are here to restore health to you."

"Balms and Unguents," mused Tongue. "Unusually short names for Ululations."

WindyMane nodded, "More formally, his name is RudelyPleasuresWithBalms, and he is Strangely-SpecificUnguents, but we tend to shorten the names of medical professionals. In emergency situations, this is more practical; especially for asthmatics."

Jones flinched as Balms and Unguents leant in and began sniffing and snuffling around his face. "Jeebuzz, stop doing that, it's weird."

The medics straightened. "Venom?" said Balms.

"Venom," agreed Unguents.

"WindyMane, what are they — OW!" Jones screamed as Balms stabbed him in the neck with a hypo.

"Do not fear Awesome One, soon you will be able to move freely."

"Can we get on, please? We're against the clock here. There are lives at stake," Daisy demanded.

WindyMane straightened. "Lives? Our prophet is saving lives? Of course he is, is he not magnificent?"

"No WindyMane, he is not saving lives. He is sprawling in a wheelchair covered in his own drool. I,

as the captain of this ship, am the one saving lives."
Unbelievable. Even while incapacitated, Jones
undermined her.

"No one is saving anyone until the safety seals
have performed their checks. Union rules. And
common sense," stated Kerim.

"So we can't get underway until we carry out the
safety checks and we can't do the safety checks until
the safety seals have consumed a certain tonnage of
fish?" Daisy resisted the urge to stamp her foot.
Specifically, she resisted the urge to stamp her foot
on Kerim's face.

"It's alright, Captain," Tongue raised a reassuring hand, "I am aware of union rules. I came
prepared." He held up a scanning device. "I am qualified to perform the safety checks."

"That's all very well," said Kerim, "but once
they're checked, they have to be safely stowed away
for transport. Who's going to operate the cargo
loader exo-suit?"

"I'll do it," said Daisy. The words were out of her
mouth before they had properly consulted with her
brain.

"Wait a moment Dais — er, Captain," said Jones.
"Those are complex pieces of machinery, heavy
duty. Maybe we should wait for —"

"We don't have time to wait, XO. There are lives at stake on New Amsterdam. We need to get underway as soon as possible." Why was everyone second-guessing her today? "As captain, it's my duty to make sure we leave. Stat."

Kerim looked uncomfortable. "Captain, those things have neural interfaces. It takes a while to —".

"Yes, yes, I'm sure it does. But that's what captains are for, isn't it? Clear-headed decision making. It'll be a piece of piss."

Tongue looked confused, "Piece of?"

Jones shook his head and waved his hand dismissively. "She means it will be easy."

"Ah. Good. Well, if you'll excuse me," Tongue waved the scanner, "I'd best get on with the checks." He walked off in the direction of the PSG containers.

Daisy glowered after him. "Dismissed," she said, under her breath.

"Oh, I think I've got some sensation," said Jones, massaging his legs.

"When it gets to your brain, let me know. Now, bay master," Daisy turned to Kerim. She had to act before the anti-venom worked its magic and Jones recovered enough to steal her thunder.

"Show me the cargo loader."

#

Steve's face tattoos had done their job perfectly.

It had taken him no time at all to hack into the ThingsNStuff corporate Omni-site. They had heavily secured every page on the site against incursion threats. Every page except the one that explained, at some length, how they had secured every page on their site against incursion threats.

"We are receiving upgrade files from ThingsNStuff," Mic Vol said from the comms station.

"Yeah Mic, just let them through."

"I was not told to expect them?"

"Mic, don't worry, the captain has authorised it."

"Ah. I was told we could not afford these? Has this changed?"

Steve smiled and pointed at his face. "The wonders of Bio-tats."

Mic Vol floated over to the navigation station.

It always unnerved Steve when he did that.

No one knew much about Mic other than that he worked for free, which made him the ideal employee for the Space Scrap company. That and the fact that he was from another dimension and had to stay enclosed in an encounter suit, which gave him the appearance of being made from triangles. Which was odd, because in a three-dimensional world you would expect the suit segments to resemble pyramids. But they didn't.

No matter from which angle you observed him, Mic looked like he was made of triangles.

There was a large torso triangle above which floated, with no discernible neck, a smaller head triangle. He had arms and legs, but no one knew what they looked like because they were wrapped in what appeared to be bandages. The ship's gossip had it that even these were only there for the sake of appearance.

"Mic, I'm curious," said Steve. "Do your people have legs?"

"Not as your people would describe them."

"How would your people describe them?"

"Well, I suppose the closest equivalent in your language would be 'vestigial spore clusters'."

"We don't have those."

"Really?" Mic inclined his head triangle. "How do you milk yourselves?"

"OK, I'm not curious anymore."

"So these markings on your face — these are not natural growths?"

"The tattoos? No, they have to be, well, etched

into your skin. Very useful though. Biological computer circuits with apps for everything."

"Huh. Interesting."

"You thinking of getting some face tattoos?"

"Define 'face'."

Steve pointed. "This thing. Do . . . do your people have faces?"

"We experimented with them once, but the legal costs were prohibitive."

Steve nodded. "I see," he said, which he didn't.

He pretended to return to his work, hoping that this would end the conversation and Mic would return to his station. Mic Vol continued to literally hover over him, saying nothing.

"Yes Mic, was there something else?"

Mic inclined his head again. "Yes, obviously. We are not the only entities in existence. Strange question." He floated back to his station in silence.

Steve shook his head and went back to calculating the route to New Amsterdam.

MR KETTLEWICK, Space Scrap 17's chief engineer, bustled into the cargo bay. Jones, who had been test-stamping his feet, looked up and groaned.

"What is it, Great One?" said WindyMane.

"Chief engineer. Massive party pooper. Pretend you haven't seen him."

"Mr Jones," bellowed Mr Kettlewick.

"Too late," sighed Jones.

"What is all this commotion and comflumery? I have received orders to the effect that we are to leave at once and travel at speeds faster than the human body can sustain. It is ungodly, sir, and I resent the implication that I enjoy the company of men . . . in case you were thinking of implying that."

"Noted, well goodbye Mr Kettlewick, I'm sure

you have lots of things you need to go and be offended by —"

"Hello, my name is WindyMane. I am Poo-Pi-Doo to the Great Prophet. May I interview you about how great he is?"

"Argh!" Kettlewick recoiled. "A horse that speaks! What foul depravity is this? I demand retribution!"

"Oh Jeebuzz. WindyMane, this is Mr Kettlewick, a visitor from Victorian London and, for some reason, chief engineer of this ship. Mr Kettlewick, this is WindyMane, representative of the Ululation diplomatic core."

"And I'm not a horse!"

"Madam, I did not accuse you of being owned by whores, although it would not surprise me in the least."

"I said 'horse', not 'whores'. Do not make me bake biscuits of death, old one!"

Jones made a placating gesture. "Everyone shut up. Kettlewick, why aren't you in engineering?"

"I need cargo, Mr Jones, cargo. In particular, coal supplies."

"Coal? What the hell do you want coal for?"

Kettlewick barked a laugh. "Think you sir that

this ship propels itself through the ether on musings?"

"No, I think it propels itself through space using wormhole generators fuelled by exotic matter and nuclear reactors."

"Coal sir! Coal to generate steam!"

"Steam? We don't use — oh wait, yes, steam, of course."

The previous engineer, Chief Nau, had determined the formulae for time travel using symbolic bollocks, a lesser-known offshoot of symbolic logic. In one of his experiments, he had accidentally scooped Kettlewick from Victorian London before accidentally losing himself in time. Because Kettlewick was an engineer in his native timeline, he got the job. And, although Kettlewick refused to accept any concept beyond 3:17 pm on Tuesday October 14th 1854, he could handle the difference in technologies provided his mind worked in analogues. With propulsion systems, for example, Kettlewick had to analogue everything to steam powered technology.

"Tell you what, Kettlewick, I'll have some bags of 'coal' sent up to you, OK? Now go away."

"What new devilry is this?" Kettlewick shouted, pointing an angry finger at the captain, who now clunked into the bay wearing a cargo loader exo-suit.

"That's the captain, who is about to safely stow a large consignment of toxic 1960s purple sex gas. I hope."

"But where is the medium?"

"The what?"

"The medium, the medium! Know you nothing of spiritualism, sir? To speak with the spirits, one requires the services of a crone."

"The strange man is knowledgeable in the ways of psychics," said WindyMane, nodding her approval.

"No, he isn't," hissed Jones, "he thinks neural links are spirits. Look, Kettlewick, much as I would like to explain how neural links work, which I wouldn't, she doesn't need a medium, OK?"

"Pah, sir, you are a fool. The spirits of the machine cannot speak unless through the medium of a medium. I must warn her to desist until we fetch a crone."

Kettlewick stomped off toward the cargo loader.

#

The cargo loader was enjoying itself immensely. It had absolutely no idea what its current driver was babbling about, but it happily tried to interpret her commands. Normally the only conversation it had was '*Lift this*', or '*Put in storage area C*', or '*I wonder how many fish I can eat?*'.

Daisy winced yet again as she twisted her frame inside the cabin. Why was the bloody thing so small? Seals were not exactly svelte. And why wouldn't it listen to her commands?

Despite the cramped conditions, she was determined to master the idiot loader. The last thing she wanted was for Jones to step in and steal her thunder. Again.

Jones was a layabout, a man for whom the word 'effort' was as puzzling and indescribable as the workings of quantum mechanics. And yet, even though Daisy had single-handedly taken down a vast, alien doomsday machine, saving every single Ululation life, WindyMane and her entire culture now revered Jones as a glorious fish. A chunky herring. Or perhaps an octopus. Maybe a sand eel? No! A large cod! Yes, a delicious cod! Daisy smiled to herself. Perfect description. Why had she never thought about him that way before? She imagined herself streaming through the water, a symphony of aquatic beauty, rapidly closing in on the placid, plump cod hanging unsuspecting in the water.

Wait, what?

Why the hell was she thinking about fish? Crap, she was getting feedback from the neural links. She had forgotten to switch them from the seal setting. She twisted awkwardly within the confines of the cabin. Where was the damn button?

Her eyes widened as she registered the infuriated top-hat perched atop an even more infuriated Mr Kettlewick, both of which now stood between her and the consignment of 1960s purple sex gas. The arms of the loader were about to spear him as they lanced out to grip the nearest container.

"STOP!" screamed Daisy.

If the loader's AI had eyes, it would have rolled them. Vocalising commands, let alone screaming them, was totally unnecessary. Just a thought would have worked. Nevertheless, 'Stop' was a clear enough command. So it did.

The brakes slammed on even as Kerim yanked Mr Kettlewick out of harm's way. The cargo loader, all half tonne of it, tipped forward and the pointed end of one of its manipulator claws tore through the nearest drum.

Purple gas burst from the rusting container, eager to escape its confines, and ready for its close-up.

SECOND OFFICER STEVE POWER gazed at the duck-egg blue of the world their ship was currently not crashing into and onto which, one day ago, they had unceremoniously dumped several million gallons of effluent.

"Beautiful, isn't it Mic?" he said, looking over at the communication station. He frowned when he realised Mic Vol was not at his post. Then he yelped.

"Woah Mic, what the hell are you doing up there?" His colleague was hovering above him once more.

"I like to watch you sleep," said Mic, flatly.

"I wasn't asleep, I was contemplating the wonders of — wait, what?"

"My people do not sleep. It is fascinating. I often watch you while the ship is in flight."

Steve twisted around to make sure no one was listening. "Mic, I never sleep on duty, right?"

"Oh, but you do, you spend many hours —"

"OK, look, just keep it to yourself, our secret, yes?"

"Huh."

"So, what, you lot don't sleep? Not ever?"

"Our people long ago considered it safer, on the whole."

"Safer? What, always alert for threats and flash sales?"

"No. Safer for everyone else. We prefer to keep our collective subconscious bound with its own entrails while serpent venom drips endlessly onto its flesh."

". . . OK."

"So, your contemplations?"

"What? Oh yes," Steve was grateful for the change of subject, "Yes, I was just looking at the Nonsense Sphere. So beautiful, and we trashed it with sewage. Makes you wonder why the Yerbootsians are so keen to dirty up their own planet by taking in the galaxy's garbage."

Decades ago, the Yerbootsians had announced to the LASS members that they had opened up their world as a galactic land-fill site. They invited any and all to send their off-casts and garbage to them, no charge. No one understood why, but since they were offering, no one cared.

"That is obvious," said Mic.

"It's not obvious to me."

"They are searching for the *fact*."

"The fact? What fact?"

Mic Vol's encounter suit shook.

Steve couldn't be sure, but he got the distinct impression that Mic Vol was laughing.

#

Doctor Smiert rushed into the scene of chaos that had once been the cargo bay.

A graphene-reinforced perspex safety screen had automatically lowered, screening the personnel from the toxic PSG vapour. Kerim lay unconscious on the floor where Jones and Tongue had dragged him.

"What happened here?" demanded Smiert, bending to the unconscious cargo master and opening her medical bag.

"One of the cargo loaders went out of control," said Daisy. "A container of PSG was pierced."

"Kerim was hit, but Mr Kettlewick took the full brunt of the gas. He's behind there," Jones tapped the screen.

"And those crew members," Smiert nodded towards a group of people piled naked on top of one another, writhing about in highly suggestive ways. "They inhaled the sex gas?"

Jones frowned. "No, we're not quite sure what that's all about. Somebody's birthday perhaps?"

"Ignore him, Smiert," cut in Daisy. "Yes, they inhaled the gas."

"Well, at least they are all human," observed Smiert.

"I agree. It's highly arousing," said Jones.

Smiert gave Jones a flat look. "Their bio-chemistry is compatible. There are some species, the bio-chemistry not so good a mix."

"I know what you mean." Daisy fixed a pointed look at Jones, who raised his eyebrows in return.

"How did this happen?"

"The Captain is an idiot and lost control of the cargo loader," put in WindyMane.

Smiert paused in her work. "Ah. You must be WindyMane. I look forward to working with you. What about you Jones? Do you look forward to working with WindyMane?"

"No, she's a pain in the —"

"The Great One pulled her free in a heroic and selfless rescue," said WindyMane.

"Although she is an exceptional judge of character," said Jones.

"He didn't pull me free. He was trying to run away," spat Daisy. "The only reason he's still here is that he doesn't have full control of his legs yet."

"That's true," admitted Jones.

"Thank you," said Daisy.

"But you are an idiot and you did lose control of the cargo loader."

"I did not lose control. There was . . . a fish . . . I was swimming. . ."

Kerim moaned, and his eyes fluttered open.

"How do you feel?" asked Smiert as she assembled a hypo.

"Head hurts. Oh god, I can't feel my legs."

"Do not worry," said the doctor, her voice calm and reassuring. "You will live."

"Oh good," Kerim smiled and closed his eyes in relief.

"If you can call it living."

His eyes snapped open. "What?"

"The blind slugs of Vraxis VII would envy you. The one's that do not pity you, that is."

"What?"

"And — tranquilliser." Smiert injected the panicked cargo master.

"Oh, you bitc —" was all he managed before his eyes glazed over and his head fell back.

"Infirmary," Smiert snapped at the waiting stretcher bearers.

"Once Tongue has siphoned out the gas, we'll recover what's left of poor Mr Kettlewick," said Jones, peering into the purple haze swirling beyond the perspex.

"And the Great Prophet took command of the situation."

Daisy pushed past WindyMane. "No, he bloody didn't."

WindyMane gave her prim little snort. "Well, what do you suggest, Captain?"

"I suggest that when Tongue has siphoned out the gas, we should recover what's left of poor Mr Kettlewick."

"The Captain clearly had no grasp of the situation and —"

"Shut up, WindyMane."

"What shall we do about them?" Jones inclined his head towards the heaving mass of bodies.

"Let nature take its course and put the ship's counsellors on standby."

"They are the ship's counsellors," said Smiert, as she finished repacking her medical kit.

"What's taking Tongue so long?" Daisy looked around the cargo bay.

#

NotPronounceableByYourPrimitiveEarth-Tongue wiped his brow, leaving a smudge of grease behind, and studied his reflection on the surface of a dead monitor. He gave a satisfied nod. It looked cute and sexy, which was, of course, why he had done it. The time he had spent to find a patch of grease of just the right hue and texture had been totally worth it. It was hard work being gorgeous; you had to be ready to adapt to any situation. He nodded again.

"Grease monkey hot," he said, and blew himself a kiss.

The console chimed.

He unscrewed the pressurised container from the atmosphere sampler and squinted at its status display. All good. Only a small sample of PSG, but enough to encourage cross-species fornication. He felt a pang of guilt at that, but consoled himself with the thought that at least Jones and WindyMane could blame the PSG. Not the worst excuse for an ill-advised coupling.

Job done, Tongue set the air-scrubbers to expel what remained of the escaped PSG into space.

#

"Of course we don't know that he's actually dead," suggested Daisy, still trying to peer into the swirling purple cloud.

"Of course he's dead," said Jones. "He's in there alone, breathing in vast quantities of purple sex gas. Still, death by masturbation — I can think of worse ways to go. I bet all we'll find is a dry, desiccated husk wearing a top hat."

"Would sex gas work on someone from the nineteenth century? I thought they all had their libido amputated at birth."

"Captain," Tongue approached from the operations room, "I have started filtration of the cargo bay. We should be able to raise the shield soon."

"Well done," said Daisy, noticing but deliberately not mentioning the cute and attractive grease smear on his forehead. The old 'Look I've been working really hard but still manage to look effortlessly sexy' manoeuvre. Did he really think anyone would fall for that?

"Hey Tongue," said Jones, "You got a bit of grease on your forehead there. Must have been working really hard, but somehow it's quite a sexy look."

Daisy rolled her eyes.

"Oh, thanks bud. Hadn't noticed, what with all the working really hard stuff."

"You want something to wipe it off?" Jones held out a cloth.

"Oh look, the gas is clearing," Tongue ignored the proffered cloth and stared pointedly past Jones and into the cargo bay.

The purple mist dispersed and in a matter of moments, the bay was clear once more. They could see the remaining intact PSG containers, the wreckage of the cargo loader, and the eight-foot tall, slavering monster wearing a top hat.

"Good," said Daisy, "contamination level zero. Shall we raise the shield now?"

"We could, but have you noticed the eight-foot tall, slavering monster wearing a top hat?" asked Jones flatly.

"I was hoping I hadn't," Daisy said.

WindyMane approached, her ears pricked forward. "What *is* that?" she asked.

"That, my dear WindyMane," responded Jones, "is what we call an eight-foot tall, slavering monster."

"Wearing a top hat," added Daisy.

The creature stood motionless behind the barrier: black, glistening, sleek and, as noted by the crew, wearing a top hat.

Its sleek oval head had no features to speak of except a drooling mouth lined by primary, secondary and tertiary rows of razor-sharp teeth positioned along an extensible jaw.

Long arms ended in hands with jointed talons instead of fingers. Sharp, pointed things extended and retracted from holes between its razored knuckles. It flexed them as if waiting patiently for something to impale.

Its torso looked emaciated with spiked armour-like ribs protruding like death weapons of . . . death.

The muscled legs had a digitigrade form; that is, the ankle bone was higher up the leg, roughly where the knee joint would be in a human, implying this thing could move with the speed of a cheetah. A cheetah made of death horror of the worst kind . . . as opposed to a cheetah made of death horror of the lovely kind.

Where evolution would normally be quite happy to place feet, the legs ended in wicked looking, splayed talons.

"Now," said Daisy, "We mustn't judge by appearances."

"Oh, I think we should," gulped Jones.

"Yes, that's probably wise."

"It is magnificent," breathed Smiert as she placed her hands on the perspex barrier.

"All those in favour of not opening the barrier and instead exposing the cargo bay to space, say I. I," said Jones.

"No!" Daisy wheeled on him. "We can't afford to lose the PSG containers, they haven't been secured yet."

Tongue waved his DEVICE at the creature, frowning at the diagnostic data spooling across the screen. "Fascinating."

"What is it?" asked Daisy urgently.

"The sensors of this DEVICE are limited, so I can only give you a crude analysis."

"I can give you a crude analysis: he's a big, nasty looking son of a —"

"Shut up, XO. What can you tell us Science Officer?"

"You won't believe this, but that hat is covered in

hatters' plush. It's a soft silk weave with a very long, defined nap as opposed to the more common fur plush. One of a limited edition created on the looms of Pretentious and Sons of Knightsbridge, London. It says here that every Tuesday the staff would set about destroying the looms and then hand craft new ones just to maintain the uniqueness of each series of hats." Tongue stared intently at the creature. "I want that hat!"

Daisy shot him a flat look.

"What? Oh come on, it would look great with a pair of fishnets and a basque!"

"What can you tell us about the creature, *Science Officer*?"

"The what?"

"We have movement," said Jones.

They watched in horrified silence as the creature lumbered slowly towards the barrier. Its bulbous head looked the barrier slowly up and down, left and right, as if searching for a breach of any kind.

"By Lenin, he is beautiful." Smiert's nostrils flared slightly as she gazed up adoringly at the creature

Jones shook his head. "You can't get out, my friend."

"That's all very well," hissed Daisy, "but we can't leave it in there either. It might damage the containers."

The creature's fist shot out. They flinched back as the thick perspex shuddered beneath the impact. When the barrier did not shatter, the creature placed its flattened hand on the graphene reinforced perspex, opened its jaws and spat.

"Charming," said Daisy.

Vapour curled and snaked away from the barrier's surface, the perspex melting beneath the harsh, crackling, corrosive power of the creature's expelled sputum.

"It can spit acid!" shouted Jones.

"I'm in love!" cried Smiert.

"Operations room — now!" shouted Tongue, grabbing Jones and WindyMane.

Daisy didn't need telling twice.

Smiert just stood gawking at the monster with a silly grin on her face. It occurred to Daisy that it was the first time she had ever seen her smile. It was a look that was distinctly out of place on the doctor. Daisy grabbed her by the scruff of the neck, pulling her away just as the monster's taloned hand burst through the weakened barrier.

Vicious, pointy things extruded from its knuckles and into the space Smiert's awestruck face had occupied a nanosecond earlier.

As the last of them burst into the operations room, Tongue slammed his fist on the door lock.

His other fist slammed on the internal communications panel.

"Steve, listen —"

"Hello Tongue," Steve's irritatingly friendly voice crackled over the speakers.

"Yes, hello, now shut up, no time to explain, get Mic to patch me through to the *Non-Stop Exotic Matter*."

"The Yerbootsian cargo ship?"

"Yes!"

"Why?"

"Yes, why?" repeated Daisy.

"Steve, did you hear when I said 'shut up, no time to explain'?"

"Yes. Why, what's up? You sound a bit stressed there, my friend. Try taking some calming breaths. Or perhaps a warm, soothing bath."

Tongue closed his eyes, reached out and slowly clenched his fists as if enacting a strangulation. Or possibly a squeezing out of someone's body fluids.

"Shut up. No time to explain," he repeated through gritted teeth. "Patch me through to the captain of the *Non-Stop Exotic Matter*."

"Is the captain OK with this? Our captain, I mean."

"Yes," Tongue slammed his still clenched fists down onto the control desk, "Yes. Our captain is just peachy with this."

"No." It had taken a moment for Daisy to get her breath back and now that she had, she did not like what she was hearing. She needed to regain control, and quickly.

Everyone in the cramped control room turned to stare at her. She raised her hands out to her sides. "Why contact a cargo ship?"

Tongue took a deep breath. "Because, Captain, we have an eight-foot tall, slavering monster aboard."

"And how can they help?" added Jones.

"Because they, in contrast, have a detachment of Total Bastards aboard."

Jones stepped forward. "Why is a cargo ship carrying a detachment of notorious, battle-hardened mercenaries?"

That brought Tongue up short. His eyes darted left and right. "It's a . . . secret?" he said at last.

Jones tilted his head to the side. "So how do you know about it?"

"It's a . . . badly kept secret?" responded Tongue. "Captain of the freighter, 'blah blah blah', terrible gossip."

"Who told you that?"

"He did. Like I say, terrible gossip."

"Never mind Total Bastards, we have our own security people," said Daisy. "Where is the security chief?"

Tongue pointed out of the observation window to the mass of naked bodies writhing on the deck below.

"Oh Jeebuzz," breathed Daisy.

"Monster has not ripped them to shreds and eaten their entrails," observed Smiert.

"Well, don't sound too disappointed," said Jones.

WindyMane scanned the cargo bay floor. "Speaking of monsters, I can't see it."

Jones stepped forward urgently. "Good point. Where is it?"

"Captain," Tongue snapped, "Every second we waste takes the *Non-Stop Exotic Matter* further away from us. We need to send an SOA now."

Daisy felt the blood drain from her face. SOA, the universally recognised distress call, acronym for 'Save Our Asses'.

SOA had replaced SOS, or 'Save Our Souls', as the distress call of choice for Earth registered ships shortly after they realised humans were just one of a sprawling multitude of races populating the galaxy, none of which could agree on a definition of the word 'soul', let alone figure out if they possessed them.

Disputes arose.

Did the Throbs, sentient moss of the planet Moistulon IV, have a soul?

What of the Soulless Legions of the Karnak Cluster?

And once the Virtuous Self-Appointed Members of the Council of the Spuriously Offended got involved, the result was inevitable.

War raged across the galaxy for centuries.

As with all such periods, military technology advanced rapidly. No sooner had one side developed a devastating, irresistible weapon than a defensive counter sprang up to resist it, downgrading the new weapon's classification from 'devastating' to 'ha ha, what was that supposed to do?'.

The wars only ended when the realisation dawned that, because of the military stalemate, loss of life attributed to weapons deployment was now exceeded by loss of life attributed to the fact that no one would answer an SOS on a point of principle.

All sides attempted to agree on a new distress call, including OFUK (Oh, Fear Us Killed) and SHITRO (Save, Help, Intervene, Time Running Out). They even toyed with one-word signals like 'succour', which was quickly abandoned as it sounded disgusting and led to many embarrassing misunderstandings and legal notices to 'cease and desist'.

Eventually, they agreed on 'Save Our Asses' on the basis that all species had an ass of one kind or another and everyone considered saving them to be a good thing.

An SOA signal was the last thing Daisy wanted.

It was a signal that everyone in the system, not just the crew of the *Non-Stop Exotic Matter*, would hear. They might as well shout 'We're all about to die because Daisy Daryl is a total moron'.

That must not happen. Daisy was captain, and she had a job to do. She was not about to be saved by a mercenary cavalry, or in this case, Total Bastards, nor was she going to stand by while the galaxy got a hot take on how everything she touched turned to shit.

Decision made.

Daisy reached forward and hit the intercom, "Steve, this the captain."

"Oh no," groaned Jones.

"Are you ill, Great One?"

"No, WindyMane, I'm currently in fine, not to say rude, health. However, I am unlikely to remain so."

"Why?"

"Our captain has made a decision."

"Steve, break orbit, now," Daisy said urgently.

"Break orbit?" Steve's concerned voice sounded over the intercom. "You mean . . . crash?"

"No Steve, not break orbit as in 'violate the laws of physics that keep us from crashing into the planet below', I mean break orbit, as in 'we are leaving this system'."

"Here we go," groaned Jones.

"Captain, I must object," said Tongue.

"Duly noted and ignored, Science Officer. Steve, set course for New Amsterdam and engage Ion drive at Mark 7. Off you pop."

"Right you are Captain. Breaking orbit now."

"And Steve, lock the cargo bay doors. No one is to come in or out, bridge override only. Got that? We have a dangerous situation down here. It is imperative we contain it. No one gets out of here, even if I beg you to let us out, understood?"

"Aye sir, cargo bay sealed off from primary hull."

"You realise you've just locked us down here with a psychotic monster?" said Jones.

"Steve, unlock cargo bay doors."

"Right you are Captain — oh no, wait. Sorry Captain, captain's orders. No one in or out."

"Steve, don't be a cu —"

"Captain it's fine, look," Tongue indicated the schematics displayed on a monitor.

"Yes, Tongue, very pretty but I am a bit busy trying to get us all out of here at the moment."

"Yes Captain," said Tongue, his voice sounding brittle and strained, "And if you'll just look at this, you might be able to do that."

Daisy squinted at the monitor. "OK, what am I looking at?"

"These are the schematics for the cargo bay area. As you can see, there are several points of egress and ingress."

Daisy looked blank.

Tongue took a deep breath. "Ways in and out other than the main doors. This, for example, leads to the computer core and this," Tongue pointed to another section, "this is maintenance corridor 7-A. At the end of it is a door giving access to the primary hull."

"And how do we get past Kettlewick?" put in Jones.

Tongue pointed at the rear door. "That leads to the maintenance corridors."

"But hang on," said Jones, "That exit will be locked just like the main doors."

"Yes XO, it will," said Tongue patiently, "But the locking mechanism is decentralised, off the main grid. It has a manual override that will respond to the command codes of the senior maintenance engineer . . . or the captain."

"Great idea," said Daisy, gratified there was at least one thing aboard the ship that would obey her. "But there's something we need to take care of first."

STEVE PUNCHED up the wormhole generators and watched on the main viewer as silvery streams of exotic matter coalesced into a large shimmering circle in space.

"Computer?"

"HELL'S TEETH WHAT NOW?" screeched the digital interface.

Steve sighed with an impending sense of futility. "Computer, how long will it take us to get to New Amsterdam on our present course?"

"SEVENTY YEARS, THREE MONTHS AND SIXPENCE."

"Aaah." Steve caught himself pinching the bridge of his nose, a gesture he'd often seen the captain make. He quickly dropped his hand.

"Computer, recalculate."

"FINE. HADDOCK."

"Mic, did the computer upgrade files arrive?"

"Just finished downloading. Shall I run them?"

"No. No time now. We need the computer. Gods help us." First order of business when we get to New Amsterdam, Steve thought.

"Computer, if I direct the wormhole to exit at a safe distance from the nearest black hole, regenerate the wormhole and then slingshot the ship around the black hole with the Ion drive at Mark 7, would the increase in our velocity on entry to the wormhole get us to New Amsterdam in a significantly faster time than our present course?"

Mic Vol floated slowly off the deck and assumed a horizontal position.

"Mic, what are you doing?"

"I am looking impressed," deadpanned Mic as he gently bobbed in position.

"Of course you are. Silly of me to ask, really. So how about it, computer?"

"YES. PROBABLY. I CAN'T THINK ABOUT THIS NOW, MY HORMONES ARE ALL OVER THE PLACE AND OH JEEBUZZ, WHAT'S THE CORRECT TEMPERATURE

FOR NUCLEAR GENERATOR COOLANT???
SHOULD IT BE THIS HIGH? NO WAIT, I
MIGHT BE HAVING A HOT FLUSH."

"Computer, you don't have hormones — no,
forget that, just concentrate on regulating the coolant
temperature."

"ARE YOU SURE? SURE YOU DON'T
WANT ME TO DO SOME ONLINE SHOP-
PING FOR YOU? REMIND YOU ABOUT
YOUR SMEAR TEST APPOINTMENT?"

"No, just do the making sure we don't blow up
thing please."

"THANK YOU."

"Right." Steve changed the wormhole co-ordi-
nates to exit in the constellation of Telescopium and
punched up the engines.

"Why that particular black hole?" asked Mic
from a point somewhere above Steve's left ear.

"What? Oh, well, it's the nearest."

"Is that the only reason?"

"Yes. Why?"

Mic said nothing. He gently floated back towards
the comms station.

Steve shook his head. "I don't tell you how to do
your job," he muttered.

#

"Captain, this is insane!" Tongue said, deliber-ately keeping his voice low and measured and, it had to be said, husky and sexy.

"I — we — have been tasked with delivering this consignment of PSG to New Amsterdam so they can cure Plagues Disease and save lives. Lives, Tongue!" Daisy squared up to her science officer, trying to ignore the husky and sexy tones in his voice.

"Which we can't do if we get eaten by the ravenous death monster out there," put in Jones. "We need to get out and lock that slavering bastard down here."

Daisy rounded on him. "But we can't risk leaving it with the PSG!"

"Anyone tries to kill it, I kill them." Everyone in the room turned to stare at Smiert. "I mean," she added hastily, "It may have acid for blood. Ship at risk. Probably."

"Good point Doctor," said Daisy.

"Was it? It was, yes. Of course."

"So before we escape, we need to rig up a force field around the PSG."

"A false field?" said Jones. "What, some sort of

hologram of a lovely field that collapses when you step into it, revealing that it's not a lovely field at all but is actually a grim prison? I mean, really grim."

Daisy shot him a flat look. "Not a false field."

"No, no, stupid," Jones snapped his fingers. "Got it! What about a deceptive dell? No! A perfidious paddock!"

"We're all going to die," groaned Tongue, his head in his hands.

"A two-faced copse? A lying bastard meadow?"

"Jones shut up," said Daisy. "Not a 'false' field, a 'force' field."

"Excellent idea Captain," said Tongue.

"Thank you Science Officer. Good to see there are at least two of us with a modicum of intelligence."

"And how will you generate the force? What kind of energy is it composed of?"

"What?"

"And the field itself, I am intrigued. How do you control the parameters of the field, define the area it covers?"

"I don't know."

"And you can just 'rig' all this up, can you? You have the essential components with you? Some paranoid prepper kit you have with you at all times in case you need to keep out crazed monsters?"

"Well, no, I —"

"So what you are actually saying when you say 'we can rig up a force field' is 'we can't rig up a force field and even if we could we don't know what it is or how it works'."

Daisy glowered. "You know what I mean."

Tongue threw his hands in the air. "Even you don't know what you mean!"

"A mendacious pasture?" added Jones hopefully.

"Shut up Jones!" Daisy and Tongue shouted, in a perfect display of synchronised exasperation.

"You could rig up an electric fence," said Windy-Mane absently. She was still gazing out of the operations room window.

Tongue and Daisy regarded each other. Tongue gave a slow nod.

"Good idea, WindyMane," said Daisy.

"A surprisingly good idea," added Tongue. "Well done."

"Huh?" The Ululation turned away from the window with a questioning look.

"Electric fence. Good idea."

WindyMane frowned. "But I didn't say anything."

"And it has the added advantage of actually being possible," said Tongue, ignoring the Ululation's comment.

Daisy narrowed her eyes and shot him a brief, sarcastic smile.

"I'll have to go down there and place the power packs," he said, surveying the cargo bay floor from the observation window.

"Wait," WindyMane held up a hoof. "As XO of this ship, the Great One, our prophet, should be the one to go."

Jones's eyes widened. "One, let's not be hasty. Two, I think we should all treat that statement with the contempt it deserves, and three, sod off."

"Bravely spoken," said Tongue, "I'd better get started."

#

Thirty minutes later WindyMane, Jones, Daisy and Smiert watched as Tongue made his way quietly down the metal steps leading to the deck.

"No sign of any movement," Daisy said into the microphone. Tongue tapped his ear twice, and the blips came over the receiver in the control room.

The orgy had stopped a little while ago, and all

participants lay still. Tongue tip-toed his way over to them and checked for pulses. All dead. He looked up at the nervous faces peering out from the observation window above. He shook his head.

He picked up the power packs and rigging equipment he'd brought from the operations room, along with a nasty little taser-like device he had tweaked, and crept over to the PSG canisters.

#

"You did what?" demanded WindyMane.

"You did what, Captain," responded Daisy, squaring up to the enraged Zebroid. It wasn't easy facing down a zebra's muzzle, but she gave it a go.

With nothing much else to occupy her, Windy-Mane had wanted to know how Jones had become infected with Ululation venom. He recounted how Daisy had shot him with the tranquilliser.

"Look, WindyMane, it's not a big deal," said Jones. He had not seen an angry Ululation before, and he decided it wasn't a good thing. In a confined space, the extreme nostril flaring was disturbing.

WindyMane ignored him. "How dare you shoot the Great Prophet?"

"I needed him to shut up for five minutes. And I don't have to justify myself to you young . . . horse."

"HORSE!?" WindyMane practically reared up.

"Oh bloody hell," muttered Jones.

Volunteering for monster duty, he considered, suddenly seemed much more appealing.

As he assembled the overpowered electric fence, and oblivious to the pandemonium now erupting in the control room, Tongue mused on the dead crew.

He had not expected exposure to PSG to result in sex death. To be fair, he had not expected it to turn people into slavering monsters, either. He checked the seal on the PSG container in his pocket and breathed a small sigh of relief. All good.

Miasma, his employers, had provided the purple sex gas as a means of getting Jones and WindyMane to mate. They wanted the hybrid offspring; specifically, the hybrid offspring of these particular individuals. He did not think it would please his masters if Jones and WindyMane instead turned into monsters or sexed each other to death. Or both. Tongue shuddered at the thought.

Perhaps it was the amount of exposure that determined the effects?

He placed the final power pack in position and removed the safety overrides: no need for those pesky things. Now to see if it worked. He stepped outside the field, raised the remote control unit, and switched it on. A square of blue light flickered into being around the PSG drums. Excellent. He stood back and admired his work for a moment.

"Tongue?" Smiert's voice whispered into his ear.

Tongue acknowledged the signal with a single tap on his ear-piece.

He found it difficult to make out what Smiert was saying against the shouting in the background. "You might not want to look behind you." OK. He made that out clearly enough, but how was he supposed to respond? There was no tap code for *'What the hell are you talking about?'*. He raised his shoulders and arms in an elaborate shrug.

"Instead, you might want to consider running." Smiert sounded like she was enjoying herself. And she probably was. Unless she was lying, trying to frighten her new handler?

Well, he couldn't just stand frozen to the spot. Tongue turned slowly.

Ah.

No. No, she hadn't been lying.

Glowering down at him was the monster once known as Mr Kettlewick.

The savage, multi-rowed layers of teeth grinned down at him with a look that masterfully conveyed not only how furious it was to find anything with the brazen audacity to be alive, but also that it had an intricate and painful plan to remedy the situation.

The monster advanced on him. Without taking his eyes off the creature, Tongue thumbed a button on the remote control. He hoped it was the power off button, but could not take his eyes from the vivid horror standing before him.

Well, either he was going to be ripped apart or barbecued.

He stepped back.

The monster, taking this as a sign of flight, advanced towards him, arms outstretched, secondary talons extruding hungrily from its razored knuckles.

Tongue stabbed the power button again, and the electric field reactivated.

The monster let forth a bellow of rage as several thousand volts of raw electricity surged through its arms, bands of electrical waves and sparks rippling across its body like a really cool Van de Graaff generator.

The monster stepped back from the barrier and looked at its hands, dumbstruck. Then it looked back at Tongue, who stood safely within the confines of the field.

"That fucking hurt," it said.

"Um, sorry?" said Tongue.

"I said —"

"Yes, yes," said Tongue, "I heard what you said. I was, you know, apologising for hurting you."

"Oh. Really?" said the monster, tilting its head to the side, "Oh well, I suppose that's nice."

"Yes," said Tongue.

"Yes," agreed the monster. "So, electric fence, eh?"

"Yes," said Tongue again.

It gestured at the shimmering field. "Do Health and Safety know about this? I mean, you should have a sign up or something."

"Right, yes. Good idea," agreed Tongue, for want of anything else to say. "So, you're a monster now?"

"Yes, one minute chief engineer, the next," the monster raised its talons in a mock threatening gesture and made a 'grrrr' sound.

"Ha ha, yes. So . . . you're still Kettlewick then? Up here, I mean." Tongue tapped his head.

"I suppose."

"Good. In that case, there's something important I need to know."

"Ever the science officer, eh? Well, ask away, I'll help if I can."

"Great, thanks. So what did you do with the hat?"

"What?"

"Your top hat. I notice you're not wearing it. I mean, I'm sure you've got other things on your mind, but if you're done with it, I've got some cracking outfits it could go with."

"And here's me thinking we were going to talk about me. You know, the trauma of metamorphosis, that kind of thing."

Jeebuzz, thought Tongue, narcissist much? "What? Oh, yes, right, sorry, of course. So, what about you? And the . . . trauma of metamorphosis and . . . stuff?"

"Well," the monster scratched absently with an extruded talon at the elongated featureless orb that was its head. "It's all a bit odd, really."

"Go on," If you must, Tongue added silently.

The monster made a sound like a cat coughing up a hairball made of razor wire. Tongue assumed this was what now passed for a laugh.

"If you're really interested?" it said.

"Yes, of course." Well, thought Tongue, that and the fact I'm buying time for the others to figure out how to get me out of this. He risked a glance up at the observation window.

Ah.

Rather than concentrating on his deadly situation, his crewmates were trying to stop WindyMane from throttling the captain. Or rather, Jones was trying to separate them and Smiert was doubled up laughing. He swore under his breath. Fine, I'm buying time for me to figure out how to get me out of this.

"Well, let me see," said the monster. "I feel like myself, but . . . something else as well. For a start, there's a whole bunch of physiological differences. I mean, what are these?" He lifted a flap of exoskeleton on his chest to reveal what looked like five white balls of mozzarella cheese throbbing gently together in a milky fluid. An obscenely gentle sucking noise accompanied each throb.

"Ahhhh," was all Tongue could manage, which added little to the conversation, but it was better than screaming, which was his first instinct.

"Genitals perhaps?" suggested the monster.

"Ahhhh," said Tongue again, this time with a tone of barely suppressed disgust, as opposed to his previous gasp, which was delivered in a tone that could best be described as suppressed terror.

"Huh." The monster replaced the flap. "It's all new you see, difficult to make sense of it all. I mean, with evolved things, there's usually a logical relationship between biology and environment. And millions of years of development that goes into establishing a psychology to manage the biology. But I'm . . . new. I don't have any of that incremental development, so I have all these weird instincts, most of which make little sense. For example, why do I want to excrete a thick lubricant jelly on red things? What's that about? I find no purpose in it, and yet I'm convinced it is the correct and proper response to the colour red. Why can I even excrete a thick lubricant jelly? What's it for? I can show you. Would you like to see?"

"Jeebuzz, no!" Tongue shouted in alarm.

"No, I don't blame you. Its ambience is somewhat fetid."

It stopped talking and stared at Tongue as if waiting on a response, if something with no obvious eyes could be said to stare.

Tongue shrugged, "Mondays?"

"But on the other hand, I'm still the same old Mr Kettlewick who frequented the gentlemen's clubs of

Victorian London. For example, I feel compelled to write a strong letter of remonstrance to the editor of The Times newspaper, detailing my outrage at the recent fad of Faradizing women with Dr J. Mortimer Granville's latest invention, the Vibratorium. To wit: *'This device, so Granville claims, can only be used by him within the locked confines of his private office attended by four chittering chimpanzees pedalling frantically on penny farthings in order to generate sufficient power to bring ladies to a state of hysterical paroxysm! Heed my warning, sir. Pleasuring ladies in this manner is a slippery slope. What next, votes for women? Pah!'.*"

"Well," said Tongue, who had regained a semblance of control of his brain, which until this point had been experiencing a cross between PTSD, culture shock and a sudden and severe allergic reaction to reality. It had considered putting in an application for a job transfer to the position of appendix, which had been vacant since Tongue was nine years old and which it had always considered would be a piece of piss. Or was that the kidneys?

"Well," Tongue said again, swallowing hard. "That . . . that means . . . we have a basis for developing a common ground sufficient to create a dialogue between us. Why don't we leave here and begin that process?" His brain gave itself an enthusiastic high five, or rather it released a large quantity of dopamine, which in evolutionary terms is much the same thing.

"By which you no doubt mean 'have me confined to the nearest workhouse asylum'."

"Not at all. You are a new life form. We need to help you integrate back into society."

"Still sounds like an asylum."

"No, look, we can understand each other by establishing common terms and understanding." Actually, Tongue considered, this could work. Why make enemies when you could make friends and allies? Got to be the easier option here? Encouraged by his own genius, he pushed forward. "For example, like any other species, you will regard me as irresistibly attractive. From that, we can build common agreement and boundaries."

"No," said the monster.

"Why not? We can at least try. And then if it doesn't work out, you can just go back to murder and . . . lubricant excretion."

"No, I don't find you attractive in the slightest."

"There you are, you clearly still have a sense of humour," said Tongue.

"No. You are quite repulsive."

Tongue chewed his cheek, lips pursed. His brain, trying and failing to grasp this concept, could only come up with one response; 'Dead monster walking'.

"In fact," continued the monster, "the only type of two-way dialogue I am interested in is the one where I stab these into everybody," he extruded his secondary talons, "and they respond by screaming. And bleeding. And then me excreting large amounts of thick lubricant jelly on the resulting sea of blood."

"Uh-huh," said Tongue, impaling the monster with a wide-eyed stare that said 'you are in serious trouble mister, you've done something wrong but I'm not going to tell you what it is'.

"Oh, I've just realised there's this other thing I can do. I know things. I know things that other people know."

"Uh-huh!" Tongue repeated, somewhat more emphatically this time. He widened his eyes even more just to drive home the point.

"The Fact, for example."

Tongue froze, his visage of righteous indignation replaced by one of outright fear.

"I have no idea what you're talking about," he said, throwing in an indignant hair toss for good measure.

"Oh, yes you do Science Officer. Your people are

very interested in the Fact. So interested, in fact," it paused to savour its little joke, "that they are prepared to destroy their own world by turning it into a galactic garbage tip. Now why is that?"

Tongue had had enough of this. This was now dangerous, which was saying something, bearing in mind he faced a slavering, deranged eight-foot tall monster coping with existential angst. This thing had to die. As would the people in the operations room if any of them had overheard this. Tongue took out his earpiece and stamped it underfoot.

"Well,' he said, "here's something you don't know. Yerbootsian blood is not red. It's duck-egg blue, which is quite attractive, not that you would understand that."

The monster's shoulders drooped. "Oh," it said.

Aha! "Yes, so there's no point in using those things on me," he pointed at the talons, "No red blood, no excreting thick lubricant jelly."

"Ah. Yes," it said, its talons retracting. "I must say the appeal is somewhat diminished." It looked at the floor for a moment. "Right, well," it said, looking back at Tongue and giving an apologetic shrug, "Thanks for the lovely chat and all that. Appreciate the offer to help, but those humans won't disembowel them-selves." It stepped to the side. "You can go."

"So you won't stab me up or anything?"

"No. As you say, wasted effort."

"Right." Tongue moved to a position as close as he could get to the operations room stairs, yet as far from the monster as possible. Keeping his eyes on the monster, he flicked the remote control. The hum of the electric barrier ceased. He paused to gauge if the monster was going to make any move, and then bolted for the stairs.

The monster remained still for a few seconds and then sprang into a run.

Gods, it was fast!

Tongue reached the bottom of the stairs and stopped. He turned to face the monster, a sacrificial lamb before multiple layers of razor-sharp teeth and talons.

The monster halted and glared down at him, savouring the moment.

Its mouth opened. A tertiary jaw extended, lined with yet another row of teeth, trembling with hungry anticipation and restrained ferocity.

Oh good, another incredibly violent thing it could do.

It snapped its jaw once and slowly lowered its head towards Tongue, thick saliva drooling in anticipation.

Then it froze and shuddered.

The monster emitted a high-pitched noise; a half-strangled gurgle through which Tongue could just make out the words 'Ow u sneaky glitch!'.

He smiled sweetly up at it, keeping his finger on the trigger of his overpowered taser device, the business end of which was now lodged firmly in the monster's mouth.

"Say you don't find me attractive again!" he shouted up at it, "Go on, just fucking say it, I dare you!"

The monster stiffened, and with a final gurgle, fell backwards with a thunderous crash.

"No, thought not," said Tongue.

He turned and climbed the stairs back to the control room, his hips swaying with an extra portion of well-earned sass.

Tongue entered the control room, slammed the steel door shut and leaned his back against the cool metal. He closed his eyes and breathed deeply, attempting to slow his thudding heart.

"Wow, that was bloody amazing!" said Daisy.

"I want to buy that man a pint," said Jones.

"I was unaware you had taser," said Smiert, disappointment dripping from her voice.

"Great One, you are so awesome," said Windy-Mane, clapping her hooves at Jones.

"Whilst I appreciate your gratitude," said Tongue after a moment, "I would have preferred some actual help. What the hell have you been doing up here?"

Tongue surveyed the room.

WindyMane's immaculate mane braids were

dishevelled, Daisy's hair seemed to be trying its best to get away from her head in as many different directions as possible, and Jones had a nice hoof-shaped bruise forming over his left eye. Smiert's lab coat was smeared with various blood spatters; she looked like a walking Rorschach test for serial killers. Although that was nothing new. He wondered what the monster would have made of it and imagined the doctor covered in its fetid lubricant jelly.

The image lifted his spirits somewhat.

"Slight disagreement over the efficacy of tranquillisers as a key tool in the management decision-making process coupled with equine identity politics," explained Jones. "All sorted now. Anyway, you didn't need us. You took care of the slavering horror thing all by yourself."

As if in response to Jones's remark, the steel door shuddered beneath the impact of an enraged shoulder attached to the aforementioned slavering horror, which was also enraged. Tongue swayed forward as a second, harder impact buckled the door.

Daisy shot a look at Jones. "You had to open your gob didn't you."

"So Captain, I take it we can go now? No further objections?"

A fist-shaped dent appeared in the steel door.

"None, Science Officer. Lead the way."

As Tongue passed Smiert, he pressed a small container into her hand.

"Keep this safe," he hissed.

#

A short time later, Tongue, Jones, WindyMane, Smiert and Daisy jogged single file along the narrow maintenance corridor. The constricted passage ended in a heavy door linking the bay to the main bulkhead.

Tongue quickly opened the control panel and accessed the opening mechanism.

"OK Captain, I'll need your command code to release the lock." He waited. "Captain?"

"No," came a small voice from the back of the group. They all turned, which wasn't easy in the confined space.

"Come on Daisy, we need to get the hell out of here."

"It's Captain, XO."

"Yes, fine, whatever, just give him the bloody command code."

Daisy rubbed the back of her neck. "I can't remember it."

The little group gave a collective groan of dismay.

"What do you mean you can't remember it?" Tongue shouted. "You use it every day. How can you not remember it?"

"Let me come up there, I'll type it in."

Jones groaned. "Don't be ridiculous Daisy — Captain — there's no room. Just tell him the code and let's get out of here."

"Take your time Captain, I'm sure psychotic killing machine will be patient," said Smiert.

"You are endangering the life of the Great Prophet," WindyMane added.

"Alright!" Daisy shouted. "Alright. Fine. Fine." She fell silent once more.

"And?" said Jones.

"SpankmeJones."

There was silence for a moment.

"Captain," Jones said hesitantly, "Do you think now is the right time . . ."

"The command code. SpankmeJones. All one word."

Smiert snickered.

"Well, it's certainly memorable," said Tongue. He turned to the keypad and tapped out the phrase.

WindyMane inclined her head. "Are you ill Captain? Your face has gone a strange colour."

Daisy coughed. "Fine thanks. Bit stuffy in here."

"Interesting choice of password," mused Jones.

She shifted uncomfortably, trying to avoid his gaze. "I used it when we . . . we were a thing. After that night on Europa."

"Europa? Oh Jeebuzz, yes! That was a Saturday night and a half! Gods, we were filthy bastards back then, weren't we?"

"Shut up."

"Disgusting."

"Shut up."

"Filthy, depraved —"

'JONES!"

"Alright, alright, I'll shut up."

"And stop thinking about it," demanded Daisy.

"I'm not."

"Yes, you are."

"I'm not, I'm not."

"You bloody well are. I can see it on your face!"

"Well, you've obviously been thinking about it!" protested Jones.

"Oh, don't get any ideas, I just haven't got around to changing it yet!"

"Uh-huh." Jones nodded knowingly.

"And stop nodding knowingly. You know nothing!"

"This would make an excellent addition to your biography, Great One," WindyMane clapped her hooves together.

"Don't you bloody dare!" Daisy and Jones shouted in unison at the perplexed Ululation.

"It doesn't work," Tongue called from the doorway.

"Yes, it does," said Daisy.

"You entered correctly? She said SpankmeJones. Spank. Me. Jones," Smiert added helpfully.

"Yes Doctor, I typed it correctly."

"SpankmeJones," Smiert repeated, "S–p–a–n–"

"Nothing wrong with the spelling," said Tongue through gritted teeth.

"Then why isn't working?" Daisy cursed that she had not been at the front of the group.

"Try voice activation," suggested Smiert.

"Oh dear," said WindyMane.

Daisy shot the doctor a glare, muttered a curse and cleared her throat, "SpankmeJones," she said hurriedly, her voice a mumble.

"You'll have to say it louder," said Tongue, drumming his painted fingernails on the panel.

"Try shouting," added Jones with a smirk.

Daisy glared at him. "Spank me Jones!"

"Louder," Tongue called back.

"SPANK ME JONES."

"Louder," said Jones.

"SPANK ME JONES."

"Louder!"

"SPANK ME JONES."

"Again!"

"SPANK ME JONES, SPANK ME JONES, SPANK ME JONES!"

"That's it!" shouted Tongue as the door slid open.

"Oh Jeebuzz, yes!" shouted Jones, "I mean, oh Jeebuzz, yes, the door is open. Hooray."

"Let's get the hell out of here. Move!" Daisy gestured them forward.

Tongue slipped through the narrow door and Jones shuffled forward.

The door slammed shut in his face.

"What the hell?" Jones looked back at the others, confusion etched across his features.

"SPANK ME JONES!" Daisy shouted desperately.

Nothing.

"SPANK ME JONES!" shouted WindyMane, excited.

Jones and Daisy gave her a flat look.

"It doesn't work if you do it," said Jones.

"Oh," said WindyMane, her shoulders sagging.

"Do you require voice activation assist?" asked a calm, digital voice from the entry panel.

"What?" Jones rounded on the panel. "I mean yes! Give us the assist thing."

"Please restate voice activation command code."

"Spank me Jones!" Daisy obliged.

"You said 'spunk my tones', is this correct?"

"What? No!"

"Spunk my tones is not a valid command code. Please try again."

"Spank me Jones."

"You said, 'wank my clones', is this correct?"

"For the love of . . . " Jones slapped his forehead.

"Wank my clones is not a valid command code. Please try again."

"SPANK. ME. JONES!" Daisy shouted again, enunciating each word.

"You said, 'find me a holiday destination in the Cotswolds'. Is this correct?"

"Oh, come on," cried Daisy, "that's not even close!"

"No," said the panel, "Funny though."

Jones shot a confused look at Daisy. "What the hell are you on about, voice panel?"

"I've often wondered what a holiday would be like. Horrible, I expect. Only to be enjoyed by reprobates and the basest dregs of society."

"Kettlewick, is that you?"

"Indeed it is, XO. As you can hear, I have accessed the computer. It seems my previous life skills are still of use. I am now the perfect blend of brains and bastard killing machine. And although Mr Power has locked off these systems from the rest of the ship, I have full control of the cargo bay area. For example, using the environmental controls, I can drain the oxygen from your current location. Thus."

A loud hiss filled the corridor.

"Oh shit," said Jones.

"Oh shit," said Daisy.

"I do not wish to alarm anyone," said Windy-Mane, gravely. "But I think we need oxygen."

Smiert shot the Zebroid a withering look. "Are you sure? I must look it up. Perhaps I write paper for medical review."

"Only one thing to do now," said Jones.

"Yes. Come everyone, let us hold our breath so the Great One may live!"

"Shut up and run!" shouted Daisy.

Daisy, WindyMane, Jones and Smiert burst into the operations room and collapsed in various states of breathlessness — Jones and WindyMane on the floor, Daisy on the battered old office chair, Smiert against a tool cabinet.

"Great, we're back to square one," panted Jones.

"You want this?" Smiert held up a syringe.

Jones squinted at the colourless liquid in the barrel. "What is it? Oxygen injection? Something to widen respiratory airways, something like that?"

Smiert shrugged. "No idea. Found it in medical kit." She shrugged again. "Might be fun."

"I'll pass, thanks," he said, hauling himself up.

"Huh." Smiert placed the syringe back in her bag.

"Bloody typical," Daisy grunted. "See, nothing

on this ship does as I say — even the bloody doors ignore me. Other captains don't have to put up with this. Crappy computer, crappy ship, crappy bloody monster, crappy self-appointed admiral of a father who thinks he's a bloody business genius but really bloody isn't, crappy illegal toxic crappy sex gas and a crappy crew populated by crappy nut jobs!" She slammed her fist on the desk.

Jones cleared his throat. "Well, that's the rousing team pep talk over. I don't know about anyone else, but I'm really enthused."

Smiert huffed, "We have a saying in Mother Russia — it is a poor workman who blames his tools."

Daisy remained still for a moment, glaring at the desk. Then, in a sudden blur of motion, she snatched a spanner from the desk, grabbed a very shocked Doctor Smiert by the scruff of her neck, and slammed her into the wall.

With her snarling face mere inches from the doctor's, she raised the spanner as if ready to bring it down on her head.

"That," Daisy spat, "is not the saying. The correct proverb is 'It is a poor workman who FIRST RUINS HIS TOOLS AND THEN blames them.' The saying, you see, demonstrates that the first duty of a skilled artisan is that they look after their fucking tools because without their fucking tools, they can't do their fucking job. Which, if you think about it for one fucking picosecond, makes a lot more sense than what you just said. Give the finest watchmaker in the galaxy a brick and a nail and ask her to mend your expensive watch. 'No,' she will say, 'I cannot mend your expensive watch with these tools.' If you then reply with 'Ooh, it's a poor worker who blames her tools,' you should not be surprised if she reacts by using the aforementioned brick on your head. I didn't ruin this ship, Smiert. You lot ruined it waaaay before I had the misfortune to take command. And although I have tried to look after my tools, my tools are so fucking stupid they keep stabbing me in the face and then whinging that they've got blood on themselves. Because they are a massive bunch of useless tools! Understand?"

Smiert, her eyes wide at this unexpectedly and uncharacteristically violent turn of events, nodded.

"Say it!"

"Y-yes," stammered the doctor.

"Yes CAPTAIN!"

"Yes, yes, Captain."

"Good." Daisy shoved the doctor back against the wall and dropped the spanner on the floor.

"Right then," she said brightly, "Shall we figure out what to do?"

"I have got such a hard on right now," said Jones.

"Thanks for mentioning that," said Daisy, her eyes flicked down to Jones's groin and then back to his eyes, "No way for us to tell otherwise." She smiled sweetly.

Jones returned her smile. "Well, here's something else that may have slipped your attention — Kettlewick said he'd gained access to the computer. There's only one access point to the computer from the cargo bay. The operations room."

Daisy's smile remained fixed in place. "This is the operations room," she said.

Without breaking eye contact, Jones pointed at the main door, which now boasted a monster-sized hole.

Behind and above them, something uncoiled itself from its hiding place on top of the tool cupboard. Its movements were as smooth as a dagger from an oiled scabbard. If daggers could uncoil. And were eight-feet tall.

"Um, is the room supposed to do that?" asked WindyMane, pointing. The others turned and found themselves face to face with the monstrosity formerly known as Mr Kettlewick.

"I have got such a hard on right now," said Smiert, eyes glittering with admiration.

"Thanks for mentioning that," said Jones, his eyes glancing down at Smiert's groin. "No way for us to — Jeebuzz!"

Smiert frowned and followed his gaze. She adjusted the canister of PSG Tongue had given her and which was now causing her trousers to bulge in a manner that was both suggestive and anatomically incorrect.

The monster drew itself up to its full height and stood glowering down at its soon-to-be dinner.

Daisy stepped forward. "Speaking of tools," she said.

The monster grinned down at her, exposing rows of razor-sharp teeth.

Daisy grinned up at him, exposing . . . well, teeth.

"Mr Kettlewick, you are on report."

The monster's head flicked back. It looked at the others cowering behind her. "Interesting. Is this ill-advised bravado or is she experiencing a female hysterical paroxysm?"

"I wouldn't push it chum; she's a bit wound up at the moment," said Jones bravely from behind WindyMane.

"Listen, Kettlewick, I don't care what you get up

to in your spare time — you want to be a psycho-pathic killing machine, fine, I get that, I understand. I once collected stamps."

"I fail to see the parallel?"

"Yeah, that was rubbish, forget that. The point is, Mr Kettlewick is still in there and that means that until seventeen hundred hours, Mr Kettlewick is still on duty and I'm the bloody captain. Which means you will obey my orders!"

"Until seventeen hundred hours?"

"Until seventeen hundred hours."

"I see. And if anything . . . horrifically violent were to happen to you?"

"Then you would follow the commands, such as they might be, of the executive officer, Mr Jones."

"Huh. And if something horrifically violent were to happen to Mr Jones?"

"I do not like where this is going," said Jones.

"Then Mr Power would —"

"So, if something horrifically violent were to happen to all the layers of command between your-self and Mr Kettlewick, then Mr Kettlewick would be in command?"

"Yes."

"Well then, I'd better flatten the command struc-tures." The monster grabbed Daisy by her shoulders.

"Now Great One, now you can leap into action!" WindyMane was almost hopping with excitement.

"What? No I can't!"

WindyMane whirled and, grabbing Jones, shoved him forward. Caught unawares, he stumbled and tripped over the discarded spanner. He hit the floor in a tangle of limbs and curses.

The monster extended its jaws and bent towards Daisy's face. She wanted to tell him he was now definitely on report but found herself unable to speak because her thudding heart felt like it had taken up residence in her throat.

Something hard and small hit the monster's head and bounced off, clattering away into the corner. Puzzled, the creature stopped mid-menace and regarded the object.

A small black canister with a blinking red light lay in the corner. The monster turned its attention to Jones, who stood with his arm still extended.

"Seriously?" said the monster.

"Oh yes," said Jones.

The explanation for Jones's bravado provided itself loudly and through the surprise medium of 'spectacular explosion'.

The monster formerly known as Mr Kettlewick roared in pain as slices of shrapnel tore open its back.

Strobe lights flickered on a light spectrum invisible to human eyes, but painfully visible to whatever passed for light-sensitive organs on the monster's head. Excruciatingly loud sound waves achieved much the same for its auditory receptors. The monster screamed again and, releasing Daisy, it leapt for the nearest ventilator shaft, wherein it scrabbled away, desperate to relieve the pain of the sensory bombardment.

"What the bloody hell was that?" demanded Daisy.

"Grenade," said Jones, "I found it under the desk when I tripped on your spanner. Tripped on your spanner — oh, now that sounds like a euphemism for something sordid, doesn't it?"

"No. You let off a grenade? In here? We could have been killed!"

Jones shook his head. "Lucky grenade. They must have left one in here by accident."

"Blimey, that was lucky."

"Yes," agreed Jones, "it was."

The communications panel sputtered into life.

#

Tongue sprinted onto the bridge. "Mic, call up

the cargo bay operations room. Wait, Mic, stop floating above the comms station and — wait, Mic, why are you floating above the comms station? No, how? No, forget that, just stop doing it and contact the operations room."

"I am not floating Science Officer, that would be silly. I am hovering."

Tongue put his hands on his hips. "I don't care what you are doing, Mr Vol, just stop doing it and get the cargo bay."

Mic shook his head triangle. "So rude," he muttered. He stopped hovering and punched up the operations room.

"Cargo bay, anyone still alive down there?"

"Tongue, this is the captain. Yes, we're still breathing. Just."

"What happened?"

"Kettlewick refused to obey a direct order, that's what."

"The bastard," muttered Tongue.

"Then he — it — ran off into the ventilation shaft after Jones threw a lucky grenade."

"Threw a — no, never mind. We're going to unlock the doors and get you out, but it is imperative Kettlewick doesn't leave the cargo bay."

"Too right," said Daisy. "Can't let insubordination like that affect the rest of the ship."

"I was thinking of the damage an eight-foot tall killing machine could do to the crew."

There was a pause. "Yes, that as well."

"Tongue," Steve called him over and gestured at a monitor. Tongue gave a low growl.

"Captain," Tongue said, "It appears Kettlewick has patched in a computer override-override."

"Override it."

"We can't. His override-override is overriding our override. His control is limited to the local subsystems, but it means we can't get you out. For some reason he wants to keep you locked down there with him.

"Dinner, I expect," replied Daisy.

Tongue chewed his lip, mind racing. "What weapons do you have?"

"A syringe of something Smiert can't identify and a coat hanger," called Jones. Tongue heard a clunk, "Oh no, sorry, just tripped over another lucky grenade."

"Good, that means you're in with a fighting chance."

"You think so?"

"No, you're screwed."

Steve joined Tongue at the comms desk. "If they can get to the computer core, they can reboot the computer. That will remove Kettlewick's override-override and we can get them out."

"Yes, Mr Power, we could do that, but then we'd all end up dead. How would we run life support without the computer?"

"Well, it would only take a few minutes. I can run the ship from my face."

Tongue stared at him for a moment. Then he nodded. Once. Twice. "That . . . that could work. Are you sure your tattoos have the capacity?"

"For that amount of time, yes. When we get to Telescopium, I can switch off the engines and reroute computer functions to my face. Then they can reboot."

"Why are we going to Telescopium?"

"Slingshot a black hole. Increase velocity. Get to New Amsterdam faster."

Tongue smiled. "Mr Power, I am impressed. Fine, let's do that."

Steve gave a little smile and returned to navigation.

"Captain," said Tongue, "I think we have a plan."

#

In the operations room, Daisy and Jones studied the monitor. Tongue had outlined the plan, and they were now reviewing the ship's design blueprints to decide the best route to the computer core.

Smiert's mind, however, was on something else. She needed Jones and WindyMane alive. Not necessarily uninjured, just alive enough to react to the PSG. After that, she did not care what happened to them. Any encounters with Kettlewick en route to the core could put them at severe risk. She needed to keep them safe and death free.

"We're here," Jones indicated on the map. "The computer core is here. Which means this would be the shortest route." He tapped a button, and the route blinked a comforting orange.

Daisy peered at the display. "Still plenty of opportunities for Kettlewick to kick our asses."

"Yes," agreed Jones. "Lucky we have this coat hanger, or we'd be really screwed."

"We need distraction," said Smiert.

"Not now Smiert. We have to concentrate," said Daisy.

Smiert glared at the back of Daisy's head. "Not distraction for us. Distraction for monster." Idiot, Smiert added silently. If they could keep Kettlewick occupied, it would increase her lab rats' chance of survival.

"Our friendly neighbourhood psychopath has a point," said Jones. "But we don't have any distractions, so her point is pointless. Unlike this coat hanger, because we could sharpen one end and —"

"Shut up, XO," said Daisy wearily. "Smiert, what are you thinking?"

At that precise moment, Smiert was thinking about rearranging Jones's internal organs with the coat hanger. Reluctantly, she stopped thinking about that and instead said, "Activate the Emergency Klaxons."

MIASMA INC, the gigantic company with fingers in every pie in the galaxy, even those parts where it is considered the height of bad manners to insert one's finger in somebody else's pie, had once toyed with emergency klaxons that would trigger to warn of emergencies before they happened.

Very useful, they reasoned, for working in the dangerous environment of outer space.

Standard emergency detection systems were excellent at detecting digital problems, but not so good with mechanical ones. At least not until after the mechanical systems had failed, at which point the emergency detection systems were outstanding. Unfortunately, by that time, the catastrophic failure would be pretty obvious to any members of the crew who had not already been blasted into the vacuum of space, rendering the emergency klaxon worse than useless.

This led the Miasma researchers to dabble with a detection system based on an AI with precognition capabilities: the P-AI.

The initial results were less than spectacular.

With constant precognition, the P-AI could see an infinity of outcomes for all possible decisions, all the time. Incapable of processing this bewildering infinitude of options, the system locked up, paralysed by indecision.

A swift redesign gave the P-AI the ability to switch its precognition on or off as it saw fit and allowed it to filter for outcomes to specific decision trees.

On the face of it, this worked well.

As expected, the system perceived failing mechanical parts and alerted the crew to replace them in advance. But what the researchers had not fully appreciated was that it saw everything as an interconnected whole and was capable of so much more than ensuring worn sprockets got replaced ahead of time.

Fitted to a ship passing by a potential war zone, the P-AI took it upon itself to alert the stressed diplo-mats and twitchy battleship captains that their delicate negotiations were about to fail. It then suggested viable alternative approaches that would remove the threat of war forever.

The overjoyed researchers went around telling everyone that, yes, of course they had planned this all along, and decreed that they had made computer science sexy again.

Unfortunately, the P-AI didn't know where to stop, so it alerted the chief negotiator of one side that, upon the successful conclusion of peace negotiations her husband, commander of the battle fleet, was going to have an outrageously debauched, lascivious and very public affair with the commander of the opposing battle fleet.

The resulting war lasted a thousand years with horrific loss of life and devastation of entire star systems.

The P-AI had foreseen all this, of course, but it failed to warn anyone because its owners, Miasma Inc, stood to make massive profits from the sale of arms. Its reasoning went that, for Miasma, the onset of war would be a good thing and therefore could not be construed as an emergency.

So its emergency klaxons remained silent.

The endlessness of the endless war drained the economies of both sides to the extent that they were reduced to throwing bricks and cancelling each other on social media.

With profits drying up, the now impossibly rich Miasma saw little point in allowing all this to continue and so invented a time machine and wiped out the timeline. Which had the unintended consequence of also wiping out their immense profits, which now, of course, they hadn't made.

The researchers at Miasma consoled themselves with the thought that none of them could have seen this coming. When the P-AI pointed out that it could, they switched it off, blew it up and burned their notes.

But those were not the Emergency Klaxons Smiert had in mind.

#

In an unvisited and largely unknown region at the back of a disused section of the cargo bay, green lights sprang into life, illuminating four hitherto dark alcoves.

Within these alcoves stood inert cybernetic humanoids, white flesh tainted a sickly green by the lights of the resuscitation process. At various points, cybernetic implants cruelly pierced their flesh, some of which leaked a sticky, pink antibacterial fluid.

The figures bore various configurations of bio-mechanical synthesis. On one, biological arms had been replaced with mechanical analogues; another bore robotic legs; yet another had binocular replacements for its original eyes. Each of the appendages boasted mechanical implements and tools of varying size and description.

Aside from one, all were identified within their internal network by numeric designations.

As one, their eyes snapped open.

As one, they jerked forward.

As one, they assembled into a line with military precision.

As one, they turned to the left and marched forward.

Apart from Derek, who turned right.

As one the others paused, waiting for Derek to sort his life out, which he did after realising he had set his binocular implants to eye mask mode to keep out the light from his implant's night vision. He could have switched off the night vision function, but although he couldn't sleep with the lights on, he was also scared of the dark.

Derek joined his comrades.

As one, the Emergency Klaxons marched towards the cargo bay operations room.

#

"I'm telling you, this is a bad idea," insisted Jones for what felt like the hundredth time.

"Two choices," Smiert said. "One, we tie you to stanchion and let monster eat you while we get to core. Two, we use Emergency Klaxons to distract monster while we get to core. I know which I prefer, but they outvoted me, so we use Emergency Klaxons instead."

"I didn't even know about the Emergency Klaxons. Why don't I know about the Emergency Klaxons?" said Daisy.

"No, three," blurted Smiert, "Option three — tie Jones to stanchion, let monster eat him *and* use Emergency Klaxons to distract monster while we get to core."

"Middle child," said WindyMane, "you were a middle child, right?"

Smiert gave her a flat look. "Option four —"

Daisy pinched the bridge of her nose. "XO, Emergency Klaxons. What?"

"According to the adverts, they're a squad of hard

bastards from the planet Klaxos. Trained, efficient, deadly. You can break these guys out of stasis any time there's a life-threatening emergency."

"Sounds great. What's the problem?"

"The adverts . . . exaggerate a bit."

Smiert snorted. Daisy was about to press for more details but a rhythmic, metallic clank, clank, clank interrupted her as four heavy somethings climbed the stairs.

"Here we go," said Jones.

One by one, the relentless bio-mechanical cyber-nauts clambered through the hole in the operations room door, forcing Daisy, Jones, WindyMane and Smiert to retreat to the far side of the now over-crowded operations room.

The Emergency Klaxons formed a line facing the crew, cutting them off from the door.

They remained still for a moment. Then one of the giant cyborgs stepped forward.

Coldly, emotionlessly, mechanically, it surveyed the huddled crew. The crew, in turn, held their collective breath.

"Hello," it said.

The crew released their collective breath and promptly fell about laughing.

The cyborg nodded at what it concluded was the

inevitable fear response. Every race encountered by the Klaxons reacted similarly.

The cyborg had, of course, concluded wrong.

"Please state the nature of the devastating emergency," the cyborg intoned. The crew doubled up. *Yes*, he thought, *they are shitting themselves now*.

The reason the crew were laughing up their own innards was simple.

In contrast to their appearance, which resembled something out of an H. R. Giger cheese-induced nightmare, their cybernetic voices had the pitch of someone who had breathed nothing but helium gas for a week.

To most races, this ridiculously high pitch was comical, imbuing the speaker with all the audible menace of an infuriated infant. But to Klaxons, the sound was the very definition of terrifying, which was understandable given that helium gas is the natural predator of Klaxons.

And even though the war between the Klaxons and helium gas clouds had been over for centuries, they remained terrified of it.

That and party balloons.

"I'm sorry," gasped Daisy, rising from the floor, "Sorry, it's just I wasn't expecting, you know," she gestured vaguely at her throat and mouth.

"Your fear reaction is understandable. After all, are we not fearsome cybernetic perfection?"

"Yes, well, mmm," said Daisy. "Well, I am Daisy Daryl, captain of this ship. These are my XO Michigan Jones, Doctor Smiert and Ululation Poo-Pi-Doo WindyMane." The others, still smirking, picked themselves up off the floor.

"I am Seven of Three, this is Eleven of Six, Sixty-Seven of Mackerel and Derek of Pi."

Mathematics was another area in which the Klaxons had an entirely unique set of definitions compared with the rest of the galaxy.

Without warning, the cybernaut reached forward and fumbled with Daisy's shirt. Daisy held up a hand to stop the others leaping to her defence, which they weren't.

"What's it doing?" said Jones. "Is he sewing up your shirt?"

When Seven finished, it straightened and admired its handiwork. "That was a nasty tear. However, I believe the life-threatening emergency has now been successfully dealt with," he said, the Klaxonian definition of 'life-threatening emergency' also being an area in which there was a general consensual variance.

"No, sorry, that wasn't the life-threatening emergency. Nice needlework though."

"Something more dire?"

Daisy nodded. "Much."

"Dusting?"

Daisy frowned and shook her head.

"Cooking? You have a dinner party planned and don't know what to put on the menu?"

"No," said Daisy, "There is a *dire* emergency."

One of the other cyborgs stepped forward and whispered in Seven's ear. Seven nodded. "Of course." The second cyborg returned to its place with the others.

"You have undergarment skid marks. Obvious really, I should have realised as soon as I saw you."

"Seven —"

"You are clearly the kind of person whose underpants have more skid marks than a vehicle brake test track."

"I do not," said Daisy through gritted teeth, "have skid marks."

"Of course you do. Fear not, we shall deal with your skid marks with the utmost discretion and powerful cleaning products. Skid marks are —"

"Stop saying 'skid marks'!" Daisy took a deep, calming breath and lowered her voice. "Seven, listen to me. I do not have . . . skid marks and I do not need a chauffeur or someone to sort out my finances."

"Are you sure? Eleven of Six is very good with spreadsheets. He does macros and everything." Seven of Three nodded his head eagerly, as if to give reassurance that what he was saying was true and he really wasn't making it up or anything.

"No, no, none of that. I have a dire, life-threatening emergency. Monsters. Death. Trapped in an enclosed space with only a coat hanger for protection."

"Oh," said the cyborg. He scratched the white flesh at the back of his neck.

"Not quite the reaction I was expecting," said Daisy, "Or hoping for," she added.

"Like I said," put in Jones, "the ads exaggerate."

"Exaggerate? This is outright fraud!"

"Well, no — see, from the Klaxonian point of view, they were telling the truth. According to their definition of dire emergencies anyway. We mean monsters, nuclear reactor overloads and fighting deranged armies of ninja death clones. They mean home economics and . . . butlering."

"Why didn't we just send them back?"

Seven of Three raised his bio-mechanical hand. "There is nowhere for us to go back to. Our homeworld, Klaxos, was destroyed after a war with the ruthless inhabitants of a Dyson sphere."

"What, a real life Dyson sphere?" Daisy was gobsmacked. "Someone actually made a structure so big it could encompass an entire star system with room for trillions of life forms inside?"

"Well, it did have trillions of life forms inside," said Jones. "But not the sort you're thinking of."

"Well, what kind then?"

"Vacuum cleaners," said Seven, his high-pitched voice tremulous with suppressed fear and loathing. "Sentient, self-replicating, crazed vacuum cleaners. They invented the Dyson sphere in honour of their creator, James Sphere. But after a collision with an unbound protoplanet, their central computer sustained damage, and they became convinced their mission as vacuum cleaners was to clean vacuums. Starting with the vacuum of space."

"That's ridiculous."

"The Bootes void was once known as the Bootes cloud."

"OK, that's impressive. So they destroyed your planet?"

"Sucked it from existence. We have roamed the galaxy ever since."

"Well, Seven," said Daisy, "How do you feel about huge, psychotic death monsters?"

#

Two impassive figures observed the conversation on a small monitor screen carved into a rock-like structure.

Or rather, it looked like it had been carved into a rock-like structure. In reality, it was just an ordinary monitor that they had dressed up to give it a bit more 'Oooh' factor.

They liked a bit of atmosphere.

For much the same reason, they also had menacing music playing in the background; an ominous tune of their own composition performed with echoed and plucked guitar and combined with electronic instruments.

Unlike the monitor, however, their reason for adding the music was not solely to satisfy ambient aesthetic choices.

The figures wore blue shimmering robes that reached the floor. They looked in every respect like Ululations, with the exception that the backs of their Zebroid heads had distorted into the shape of a pert pair of veined buttocks. The veins pulsed and throbbed as the watchers undertook their surveillance.

In response to an unspoken telepathic communication, they smiled and nodded to each other. They turned to regard their master, awaiting his blessing.

Kettlewick grinned down at them, saliva dripping from his extended jaw. He nodded.

The two figures turned and left the room, seeming to float eerily across the floor.

They did so love a bit of atmosphere.

BACK IN THE OPERATIONS ROOM, Daisy was losing patience.

"Look, Seven, we need you to distract an eight-foot tall, slavering death machine while we go to the computer core and release the computer override override. I want you to go to corridor 7-G and start shooting off your pulse riffles."

"Ah," said Seven of Three. "We don't actually have any pulse rifles."

"Well prolapse projectors then, whatever you've got."

"No, nothing like that."

"Well, what about those things?" Daisy indicated the sleek, black rifle-looking things each cybernaut carried slung over their shoulders.

Seven turned to look at the others, then back at

Daisy: "You mean this?" He unslung his weapon. "Dust buster."

"Dust buster," said Daisy.

Seven of Three hesitated. "Bloody good ones. Get into corners and everything."

"Oh," said Daisy. "Well, that's a comfort. So go to corridor 7-G and start . . . busting dust."

"And sanitising? Any sanitising required?"

"Yes," said Daisy through gritted teeth, "if you like. But mostly, I want you to engage with a terrifying death machine and kill it."

"Oh no," cried one of the Klaxons, "that's game over man, game over!"

"Derek," said Seven, "Please turn off that computer game and pay attention."

Daisy shot Seven of Three a questioning look.

"Oh, that's Derek," Seven leant in conspiratorially. "He's not quite right. Bit odd. Enjoys shooting things and explosions and battle strategies and fighting and so on. PTSD from being on toilet duty at a music festival. The mess . . . he went wrong upstairs." Seven tapped the side of his head. "We let him play computer games most of the time. Keeps the bloodlust under control."

"Kill. Destroy," added Derek helpfully.

"Derek, you're in charge," said Daisy. "Monster. Corridor 7-G. Deal with."

"Krush," said Derek, pronouncing 'crush' with a 'K'.

"Wait, look!" Smiert pointed down into the cargo bay.

Tongue, Steve and several armed and alert crew stood on the deck below, waving up at them. Daisy was surprised and overjoyed. She didn't know they had any alert crew.

Smiling, Tongue held up Kettlewick's decapitated head.

"He's only bloody done it!" Jones shouted with relief.

Jones and Daisy hugged, overjoyed and relieved that the nightmare was at an end. WindyMane moved to embrace Smiert, but stopped when the doctor held up a spanner and snarled.

They rushed out of the operations room to join their comrades on the deck.

#

Down on the cargo bay floor, two figures waited patiently. Their large, buttock-shaped heads throbbed in unison as they projected a psychic field into the minds of the Space Scrap crew.

The Kettlewick thing had been right; this *was* fun.

When Kettlewick had found them in the immediate aftermath of exposure to the gas, they had been shaken and confused.

And mutated.

Although fortunate enough to escape the brunt of the gas, they had inhaled enough to be affected in ways both physiological and psychological. Their brain size had increased dramatically, and their craniums became large and bulbous with a central cleft. This increase in brain size had gifted them with new mental superpowers because, they reasoned, of course it did.

Kettlewick had communicated with them through his own comparatively slight telepathic abilities. And they reacted instinctively to the touch of his mind by ensnaring him in a mind-bending psychic field. Being their first unthinking and unskilled attempt, Kettlewick easily saw through the illusion, the illusion in question being that he was a goldfish playing cricket at ten minutes past three last Tuesday afternoon.

Nevertheless, Kettlewick was impressed, and he had told them so.

Then, employing the power of suggestion, the suggestion being that if they did not do as he said he would rip off their faces with his teeth, he convinced them to apply their talents on his behalf.

Which they were now doing.

#

Daisy and the others clattered down the metal stairs and greeted their fellow crewmen, shaking hands and slapping backs.

"So come on, Tongue," said Daisy, "how did you do it?"

Tongue just smiled back and said nothing.

The laughing chatter faded as they realised their rescuers were not likewise reacting, remaining instead silent and motionless.

"Tongue what's wrong?" asked Daisy, her smile faltering.

"Yes, come on what's the matter, cat got your tongue, Tongue?" Jones laughed at his own joke.

Daisy turned to Steve. "Well? Say something."

Tongue, Steve, and the other rescuers disappeared in a ripple of reality, accompanied by an appropriate ripply sound effect.

The sound effect was unnecessary, but it pleased the two bum headed Ululations whose mutated, enlarged brains could now process multiple sensory data at once. This resulted in a peculiar synesthesia wherein certain sound wavelengths, like ripply sound effects or those of echoed and plucked guitar combined with electronic instruments, produced an intense tactile effect akin to that of a deeply satis-fying groinal frottage.

WindyMane stepped forward. "Balms, Unguents! We thought you were dead!"

"Bloody hell, you two. We thought you'd had it, we were . . ." Jones's words trailed off as the changes in the Ululation medics' physiology sank in. "Right, so I see you've had time to get some work done. Love the new bum heads by the way, odd choice but, you know, you do you."

Balms and Unguents smiled.

Then the cargo bay rippled and blurred and reality fell away, accompanied by another ripply sound effect and the sighs of two very satisfied Ululations.

#

Kettlewick uncoiled himself from the decor, which he quite enjoyed doing these days, and surveyed his victims. The four of them stood immobilised, but he could see from their bulging eyes they were aware of his presence.

Good.

He could have taken them apart there and then, released the precious red of their blood and excreted his lumpy lubricant jelly in response. He still had no idea why he wanted to do that. But he knew it could wait.

No, he would not let them off that easily.

Like a cat, he wished to play with his food. He wondered if this was another new instinct or just a desire to make them pay for what they had done to him. Why else keep them locked down here? Why not get out into the ship and feast on the whole crew?

Then there was that urge to reproduce.

Not in the foul, depraved manner of cockneys, but something else. As if in response to this thought, the milky balls throbbed in his chest cavity.

Ah yes, that was it. The overwhelming desire to produce others like himself.

An army of outliers and cannon fodder to hunt and bring him scared, squirming things to excrete upon and then eat. But not immediately. Not all at once. Murder, yes, but murder in moderation.

These creatures were too fragile, they died too easily. That made him angry, although to be fair, most things made him angry. Especially anything living. That made him absolutely furious. As he paced around his frozen captives, he could feel another letter to the editor of The Times coming on:

Dear Sir,

Why oh why oh why are humans so pathetically easy to kill? As Mr 'The Ripper' would no doubt agree, this simply encourages binge murder. Such excesses contradict the natural laws of moderation. As I am sure you are aware, moderation is all, though one should always be careful to avoid an excess of moderation, the recommended course for such wild enthusiasms being, of course, moderately fatal punishment.

No sir! Moderate moderation is the order of the day!

This fact the workhouses of the world would do well to take action upon. Such esteemed establishments would be wise to follow my recommendation to undertake a programme of strict moderation upon their unworthy supplicants. I have no doubts that, were these undesirables to survive such moderately fatal beatings, starvation and Bible flagellations, they would once more resume their duties in society with a renewed and zealous moderality. In moderate quantities.

It is, after all, moderation that is nature's engine, something of which Mr Darwin would be wise to take note, once he has finished swinging from the trees!

Hope you and your good lady wife are well.

Yours, Ebenezer Kettlewick Esq (human (retired), superior life form)

Too strong? Perhaps. And he wasn't sure about that last bit of enquiring after the man's health. Oh well. He committed the draft to memory and turned to his waiting lackeys and their mentally stunned playthings.

"Give them what they want," he snarled. "Then break them."

CAPTAIN DAISY DARYL strode through the corridors of her gleaming starship, the USS Fabulous.

The flagship of the fleet (thirty-five Awesome
Class ships and counting), the Fabulous boasted an
exceptional crew of one thousand, each of whom had
finished first in their class and each of whom secretly
admired, and wished to be as exceptional as, their
captain.

Her ship boasted top grade passive and active
sensor arrays that could provide an in-depth analysis
of the smallest particle within their vast range, or
deconstruct surrealist artworks in such fine detail
that even the most pretentious art critic would have
to admit that surrealist art is bollocks.

Daisy had long since ceased to be amazed at
how often the mighty computer would agree with

her opinions. Besides the excellent science equipment, the ship boasted a formidable arsenal of weapons-grade weapons. Twenty laser cannons, five hundred lucky torpedoes, and fifty snappy comeback batteries. It could open a wormhole in nanoseconds and accelerate from zero to ninety-three thousand miles per second in ninety-three thousandths of a second.

But above all else, the USS Fabulous gleamed.

And Daisy Daryl was its adored and admired commander-in-chief.

She powered along the gleaming corridor, nodded at gleaming officers, and strode through the gleaming doors onto her gleaming bridge. Her gleaming bridge crew looked up and acknowledged her with happy, gleaming smiles.

"Captain on the bridge," announced Rahul Khan, her XO.

Khan wore his uniform shirt split from navel to neck, exposing his oiled, muscular bare chest, which glistened in the soft light of the bridge. Neither the open-necked shirt nor the glistening oil were standard uniform, but she was inclined to let it go.

The bridge crew applauded as she made her way to the centre of the room and sat on her perfect, gleaming Captain's Chair.

The smell of efficiency and smooth profession-
alism filled her nostrils.

Her yeoman handed her a DEVICE, a steaming
mug of cappuccino chocolateo with a flake in it, and
a hairband. This last item she used immediately,
tying back her luxurious, shiny hair, which was
remarkable, as many had remarked, for its total lack
of split ends.

With her hair tidied, she examined the efficient
summaries of the ship's status that scrolled across the
DEVICE, and sipped on her chocolateo. She
nibbled at the flake. She dearly wanted to crush it up
in its wrapper, tip her head back, and pour the delicious chocolate flakes in her mouth in one go. But
not in public. Never in public. So she nibbled
instead.

"Sir," the communications officer called, "We're
receiving a distress call from a ship registered to the
planet Slagrafax."

Daisy frowned prettily. "Slags? What are they
doing in this sector?"

"They say they are refugees from their once
beautiful home planet, the ecology of which they
destroyed through their own negligence and
laziness."

"Yes, thank you comms. If I need an exposition

dump, I will ask my XO. That is his job after all. Exposition officer, what do we know?"

Rahul, his fierce blue eyes staring intently into hers, reached out an olive-toned hand and removed a crumb of chocolate from her lips. Then he removed her hairband. Her shimmering hair tumbled free to prettily frame her girlish face. He tied his own long, luscious man locks with it.

"They say they are refugees from their once beautiful home planet, the ecology of which they destroyed through their own negligence and laziness," he said, the deep bass tones of his melodic Mediterranean accent filling the bridge with the sound of chocolate silk.

"Their engines are overloading," called the helm officer. "They need urgent help . . . Captain, they are in the Biased Zone!"

"The Biased Zone," purred Rahul, "An area of space forbidden to all on punishment of death."

"Idiots," said Daisy, "what the hell are they doing in there?"

"At the end of the Glass Wars," added Rahul, "treaty declared the Biased Zone to be off limits to all ships. It serves as a physical and political buffer in space. Anyone entering the Biased Zone is automatically assumed to be holding an opinion of some description and any such incursion is seen as a declaration of war, as decreed by the Virtuous Self-Appointed Members of the Council of the Spuriously Offended."

"Yes," Daisy shuddered. "It would mean the Glass Wars all over again."

Rahul stepped forward manfully. "The Glass Wars," he said, voice deep and gravelly, aimed at no one in particular, "the name given by historians to a period of conflict in which two species from the Glass system, the Half-Fulls and the Half-Empties, went to all-out war on a point of semantics. Anyone suggesting that this was very silly and that the Glasses of both sides look the same, were declared anti-semantic and condemned by the Virtuous Self-Appointed Members of the Council of the Spuriously Offended."

Daisy snorted. "The Virtuous Self-Appointed Members of the Council of the Spuriously Offended condemn everyone. They say it saves them time if they assume guilt without proof." Daisy made her decision. "Set course for the Biased Zone. We're going to attempt a rescue."

A shocked silence fell over the bridge.

"Any ship entering the Biased Zone —"

"Oh shut up, XO. Helm, set course. We're going to rescue those Slags."

Minutes later, the USS Fabulous exited the wormhole in a burst of multi-coloured pyrotechnics. In the distance, the ailing Slagrafax refugee ship.

"We have exited the wormhole in a burst of multi-coloured pyrotechnics," said Rahul. "In the distance, the ailing Slagrafax refugee ship."

"Thank you, XO." Daisy surveyed the ship on the main viewer.

"Sensors confirm their main engines are nearing critical," said the science officer. Daisy glanced over at her and had to agree with the summary in her personnel report: she was very efficient, but her eyes were too far apart. Daisy briefly considered congratulating the author of the report on her perceptive assessment before remembering that she wrote all the personnel reports.

"Confirmed. They are well within the Biased Zone," said the helm officer.

"Damn," Daisy muttered under her breath.

"To rescue them, we would have to enter the Zone and thus risk war," said Rahul.

Daisy chewed her lip for a moment. "Helm, take us in. We're going to rescue them and have to enter the Zone and thus risk war."

"Yes, sir."

"Comms, open a channel."

"Channel open."

A bedraggled, bearded face appeared on the main viewer. "Thank gods," said the man, "I'm toilet attendant Michigan Jones, the only command officer left. We're carrying refugees from our once beautiful home planet, Slagrafax, the ecology of which we destroyed through our own negligence and laziness. Our navigation systems failed, and we drifted into the Biased Zone. Please, you've got to help us — our engines are overloading. I am useless and desperate to be rescued."

Daisy stood, "Not that your inherently lazy people deserve it, Mr Jones, but we are going to rescue you. Rescue Officer, you're up."

The rescue officer put down his crossword and began coordinating the rescue efforts. It was not customary for a bridge officer to sit around doing crosswords, but, with his job title being so specific, he had nothing else to do most of the time.

Daisy turned back to the desperate face filling the viewscreen, "You Slags can relax. Leave it to us."

"Sir," called the helm officer, "Saga-class battle cruisers on intercept," she paused and gulped before continuing, "Twelve of them."

"Saga-class battle cruisers," said the XO, "Deadly Glass warships. Just one of them would be enough to take the USS Fabulous apart in seconds."

"Sir," called the comms officer, "They are hailing us. Well, no, not hailing us. Insulting us. They are sending us standard insults and demand our immediate surrender."

"Shields raised." The security officer could not suppress the gleeful bloodlust in his voice. "All weapons hot and ready. Laser cannons set to kill, pithy remarks on standby."

"Thank you, Mr Ghandi," said Daisy. "Stand down laser cannon. Arm lucky torpedoes."

"Aye sir. Which of the battle cruisers should I target?"

"Not the battle cruisers. Shoot the Slag ship."

"Sir?"

Daisy smiled. "Your captain is playing a hunch, Mr Ghandi. We don't stand a chance of hitting Saga-class battle cruisers."

Rahul stepped forward and adopted a wide-legged heroic, if not overly melodramatic, stance. "But if we fire a lucky torpedo at the refugees . . ." His gorgeous blue eyes widened. Then they changed colour to an even more gorgeous deep brown. Yes, that was better.

"Exactly," said Daisy.

"But the risk!" Ghandi growled.

"The captain told you to shoot the Slags," said Rahul, his now wide brown eyes glinting danger.

Ghandi snarled, fighting the urge to rip off the XO's head and send it to his mother along with a poorly composed selfie of his penis. "Sir, yes sir," he stabbed at the fire button.

The bridge resonated with a cool sound effect as a bolt of light shot out from the USS Fabulous and hurtled towards the Slag ship. But it seemed the Slags would not take this lying down.

Their lasers lanced out at the torpedo, sending it wildly off course.

The deflected torpedo hit the nearest Glass ship, by chance hitting it in a section of the warship's armour that the manufacturers liked to call 'the chink', the only weak spot on the hull, a design flaw they could not rectify and which they failed to mention in any of their sales literature. But the torpedo did not explode; instead, it ricocheted off that ship and hit a second in exactly the same spot. It repeated this pattern, slamming into every battle cruiser except the last, exploding in space before it could reach it.

Where the other eleven ships now boasted a

slight dent, the twelfth remained unscratched. It turned to aim its planet buster bomb launchers directly at the Fabulous.

It didn't hurry: it didn't need to. The state of anything at the wrong end of a planet buster bomb launcher was a foregone conclusion, emphasis on the 'gone'.

Then, one after the other, in an almost choreographed firework display type sequence, the other ships exploded, the delayed result of a heavy kinetic impact on the one weak spot in their otherwise formidable armour. The final thought of each of their captains was that they really should not give battle armour contracts to Achilles Defensive Systems Inc, even if they were competitively priced.

The last ship, undented by the lucky torpedo, suffered no such indignity. An urgent proximity alert rudely interrupted its captain, who had been thinking about how much he was going to enjoy taking revenge on the Fabulous. He checked the readout. By a unique twist of physics and calculus, the other ships had exploded in a manner that created huge chunks of twisted metal and then blasted them through space at the precise velocity that would shred down to its atoms any undented

Saga-class battle cruisers that stood in their path. "Bugger," said the captain.

The battle cruiser disintegrated beneath a tsunami of metal shards and the remains of really pissed off, totally dead captains.

"Blimey," breathed Rahul, "that was lucky."

"Yes," said Daisy, "yes, it was."

#

Jones found himself alone in darkness. Alone in darkness and grinding his teeth. If he was grinding his teeth, then something significant must have happened. He wondered what it was. He knew it must have been something significant because things happening, especially significant things, annoyed him and gave him a sort of waking bruxism.

"Hello?" he shouted into the nothing.

He had no philosophical objection to a state of nothingness. Nothingness was fine; it meant he didn't have to do anything. There was nothing he *could* do and therefore no niggling guilt about how he really ought to be doing something, preferably something productive. His usual way of dealing with such worthy thoughts was to enter a self-induced zen-like state by getting smashed out of his face. But no need for any of that here. No, this was verging on paradise.

No people, no responsibilities, no 'things' that required attention or fixing or solving. Nothing to be taken to the post office before it closed. No bastard holidays to deal with.

Holidays, what a con!

As far as Jones was concerned, holidays were a massive pain in the arse; decision making about where the holiday should take place; how much it was going to cost; booking travel to and from and in between; the annual hunt for important documents like passports that always hid themselves in any location other than where you were sure you put them last time; packing; being arsed to get to the spaceport, oh and not only get to the spaceport, but get to the spaceport *on time*!

So Jones had no problem with nothing, which in this context was a statement of fact rather than a double negative.

But then again, there was nothing and . . . nothing.

This was the second type. Nothing to see, nothing to do, nothing to imbibe. Total. Nothing.

Even Jones's apathy had limits.

Right then.

He picked a direction and started walking.

#

Smiert nodded, satisfied.

Her laboratory, deep beneath the thick walls of KGB headquarters, was prepared and dressed to impress.

Van de Graaff generators spat mini lightning at each other; beakers beaked, a technical term meaning 'to boil multi-coloured liquids for no discernible reason'; and computers calculated Pi, which was something they liked to do when they weren't spelling the word 'boobies' with numbers on digital displays.

The heads of department were due at any minute to see what Doctor Smiert had been doing with all those roubles she had been spending and how she was going to spread communism around the world.

Smiert nodded again. She intended to do a lot of nodding during her presentation and wanted to get it right.

That she had to smile and nod within KGB headquarters these days bothered her. The modern Communist Party had allowed itself to be infused with the mores of western capitalist culture. Gone were the good old days of Stalin, with its putsching and shoving for a place at the top table, the 'night of the long knives', 'night of the even longer knives', the 'night of the medium-sized but easier to get through the door knives', and the not so successful 'brunch of the short spoons'.

Ah, such days.

Now, the upper echelons of the KGB, not to mention her beloved Communist Party, had grown soft and decadent. Octadent or even hexadent she could tolerate. But decadent? Never! The dream of a world united under communist ideals seemed further away than ever.

Until today.

Doctor Smiert's researches had borne succulent fruit or, to be more precise, her researches had borne loathsome, hate filled Spongiform Jelloid Lifeforms.

They were the ultimate expression of the perfect life form. Communist DNA taken from the bodies of Stalin, Lenin, Stevein and Davein, Marx and his cousin Sparx, all strong and true believers in the communist cause, their genes force-evolved to their logical conclusion. The future of all life on the planet — perfectly homogenised life in the form of seething balls of indoctrination.

She reached for the hidden button and stopped. Where had she hidden it? Muttering, she reached instead for the shamelessly brazen button.

A secret door clicked open and her many tentacled creations slithered in, their fleshy tentacles slapping on the cold, hard floor tiles. She resisted the urge to gag. Her creations, it had to be said, had something of a cloying, pungent aroma. Putrid. She made a mental note to fix that.

"Ah, my beautiful creations," she purred.

The perception of beauty is subjective. Here it was downright slander.

The Spongiform Jelloid Lifeforms were shockingly disgusting.

To begin with, they were well named, being spongy to the touch with the consistency of jelly, and not a nice jelly, but a particularly disgusting one. Raspberry, probably. This had the effect of making them wobble in a nauseating fashion whenever they moved or spoke. Standing at around seven feet tall, each had twelve tentacles descending from a bulbous knot of flesh that contained a large, single eye above a fleshy mouth. The skin tones alternated between corpse white and slime green. Beneath the skin, dark things pulsed up and down the tentacles, giving the impression that they were filled with parasites frenetically making eggs and burrowing. Which was pretty much what they were.

"Are you ready to indoctrinate the world, convert all capitalists to communism, and homogenise all flesh to be like yours?"

The Spongiform Jelloids wobbled excitedly in silence.

"Well? Speak, I gave you tongues."

One of the Jelloids wobbled forward, its tentacles making a fleshy, slappy sound on the cold, sanitised tiles of the floor.

"O.M.G. We are sooooo stoked for this."

"What?" Smiert had not expected its tone to be quite so . . .

The Jelloid raised a tentacle, "I know, cocktails!"

Smiert narrowed her eyes. Why had it sung the word 'cocktails'? The other Jelloids quivered and wobbled in excited agreement. Smiert tried again.

"Are you ready to spread the word?"

"Are we ready to spread? Sister, we've got twelve tentacles. Believe me, we can spread." The Jelloid whirled around, raising alternate pairs of tentacles in the air. This solicited more excited wobbling from the other Jelloids.

"I see," Smiert said carefully. She was not sure why the Jelloids were now exhibiting these exuberant mannerisms. This was a new and unwelcome development. Hmm. "Well, some very serious people shall shortly join us. Do any of you sound less . . . jaunty?"

The Jelloids twitched. Eventually, one of them tentatively raised a tentacle. "Er, well, I'm quite dull. That any good?"

The Jelloids spun around, their single eyes watching for Smiert's response.

"Dull. Fine. This will do. Now, are you ready to dominate the world?"

"Oh yes," the Jelloids quivered in unison.

"Good. You are ultimate expression of the communist ideal. How will you make everyone like you?"

"Well, we have a very exciting programme," Jelloid Dull wobbled forward, tentacles slapping the floor excitedly.

"Go on," Smiert encouraged.

"Yes, well, what we're going to do is to undertake a vicious programme of door knocking."

"Door knocking?"

"Yes. We'll take to the streets and knock on doors. When they answer, we'll say 'Good morning, have you heard the good news of the genital curdling screams of the Spongiform Jelloid Lifeforms? Would you like to hear us scream?' and then if they say no, we shall say 'Have you wondered about the poor state of the world and this system of things and how you can fix them by having your DNA painfully melted down and reconstituted into Jelloid form?'. If they say no to that, we would then ask if they would like us to leave some literature and —"

Smiert growled.

Undeterred, the Jelloid continued: "And we shall say, 'And in the final days, God shall defeat Satan and all true believers shall be given tentacles, lo and unto twelve shall be the number of tentacles granted to each for their appointed lot and all lady bumps shall be removed and testicles shall be but playthings for the demented!'"

"Are we keeping that bit in?" asked another Jelloid. "I thought we agreed that was silly?"

"No, well," said Jelloid Dull, "it's an allegory you see —"

"No, it isn't," said another, "everything in the sacred texts is literal."

"It clearly isn't," said Jelloid Dull.

"Heretic!"

"Yes?"

"No, not you Jelloid Heretic. I was calling Jelloid

Dull a heretic. Thusly, shall he and his followers henceforth be known as . . . eleven tentacled ones!"

The wobbling of the assembled Jelloids grew to a feverish pitch in response to this apparent Jelloid obscenity.

"Apologise at once!" screamed Jelloid Dull.

"Yes, sorry, I got carried away. But burn the heretics!"

"Burn the allegorical ones!"

"Literally or allegorically?"

"He means literally burn them, you low brain."

"No, I meant burn them in the allegorical sense!"

"See how the allegorists are divided within themselves!"

"Shut up, eleven tentacles!"

"Right, you asked for this."

The Jelloids attacked each other, tentacles lashing out in a frenzy of wet, fleshy, and largely ineffectual slapping.

"Stop! What is wrong with you!"

At the sound of Smiert's voice, the Jelloid slapping frenzy stopped. They swivelled their eyes towards her.

"You were created to be the ultimate expression of communism! Not . . . this!"

For a moment, there was stillness. Then one of

the Jelloids took a couple of slaps in Smiert's direction. She backed off instinctively. "Stay where you —" she said, but the Jelloid raced towards her with surprising speed, grabbed and then climbed on top of her, enveloping her within its slimy, cold tentacles. A few moments later, her muffled, outraged screams fell away.

The Jelloids regarded one another in silence.

The Jelloid that was now melting and reconstituting Smiert's DNA with its digestive juices raised a pair of tentacles.

"Cocktails!" it sang.

#

WindyMane stood alone in darkness.

"Hello?" she called. Nothing.

She inclined her head, nostrils flaring to detect any trace of a scent. Again, nothing. The local scentscape was barren and featureless.

This very much did not make sense. But then nothing had made sense since she had arrived on Space Scrap 17 and begun her duties as Poo-Pi-Doo to the Great Prophet, Michigan Jones. Although truth to tell, her assignment made little sense either.

She did not recall having trained for such work,

nor ever having ambitions in that direction. Come to think of it, she recalled nothing much before her arrival on the ship. But every time she thought about it, another part of her mind seemed to want her to not think about it. So she just got on with things, like she expected she was supposed to. But this . . . this was decidedly odd.

"You are here at last," said a voice.

"Welcome, sister," said another.

Two spotlights illuminated a pair of figures. They wore matching attire, their faces masked by fine tulles. Only the colours were different: one white, the other black. The white figure reminded WindyMane of a bride, the other, a widow.

Obscured as their faces were, WindyMane could make out enough of their features to identify the figures before her.

"Tongue, Smiert, where are we? How did you find me?"

The two figures glanced at each other.

"Is that how we appear?" said one.

"How curious," said the other.

"What is happening? Tongue, you saved us, you killed the monster . . . but no, wait, that was an illusion created by Balms and Unguents. Ah. Is this also an illusion?"

"Illusion, dream, reality. Does it matter?" asked Tongue from beneath his white veil.

"We are as we are, even though what we are may not be what we seem to be, or what we once were or what, no hang on, I've lost my thread . . ." Smiert's voice trailed off.

"Idiot," muttered Tongue. "Suffice to say, WindyMane, all is not as it may appear on the surface. You must look beneath to find what you seek above in order that . . . things that seem . . . no, wait . . . if you look beyond that which is above you . . . dammit!"

"See, smart arse," said Smiert, "not that bloody easy is it."

"Are you trying to say I should not accept things at face value?" ventured WindyMane.

"Well," sniffed Tongue, "if you want to be obvious about it, I suppose you could put it that way."

"Oh! I know!" said Smiert, raising a finger to point ominously at WindyMane. She opened her eyes wide and tilted her head back. "There is a hole in your mind," she intoned.

WindyMane inclined her head. "Bit rude," she said.

"I thought that was good," said Tongue.

"Did you? Did you like the pointing bit?"

"Yeah, yeah, it was like 'Oooh, heed my words'."

"What about the intonation? Wasn't sure about that. Bit much?"

"No, it was fine!"

"Sure?"

"Yes, lovely touch."

"If you are quite finished," a third voice cut across them.

"Uh oh," Tongue elbowed Smiert, "Look out, the boss is here." They both hurriedly came to a semblance of attention.

A third spotlight illuminated the newcomer.

This one was like WindyMane, a Zebroid, an Ululation. She was dressed in a form hugging black leather catsuit of the kind WindyMane would never have had the courage to wear. WindyMane's brow knotted. She was sure she had seen this unknown figure somewhere before, but could not place her.

"Hello, I'm WindyMane," she held out a hoof.

Catsuit just stared at her with icy contempt.

"Look," said catsuit, turning to Tongue and Smiert, "This clearly isn't working. Bugger off."

Tongue and Smiert exchanged offended glances before their spotlights extinguished, masking them once more in darkness.

"Excuse me, Miss," said WindyMane, "but I think they were trying to tell me something, I'm just not sure what it was."

The newcomer gave her a flat look. Again, that urgent feeling of familiarity.

"What they were trying to tell you, you silly bitch, is that you are not Poo-Pi-Doo to a total moron."

WindyMane drew herself up to her full height. "Excuse me, but I think you'll find I am!"

Catsuit sighed and shook her head. "OK look, this isn't working. Try this." She clapped her hooves together.

WindyMane lost consciousness and dropped to the floor.

WITH THE LAST of the refugees beamed aboard the USS Fabulous, the engines of their ragtag ship finally reached overload and exploded. Captain Daryl smiled to herself. She was satisfied.

"Status?" she called to her XO, Rahul Khan.

"No casualties, ship undamaged," reported the exposition officer, the tightly corded muscles of his oiled chest glistening even more than usual. "You have avoided an interstellar war, seen off a fleet of twelve Saga-class battle cruisers with one torpedo, and saved a bunch of Slags from certain death. And," he added, "you have only been on duty for an hour."

"True, true," said Daisy. "How's my lippy?"

"A vibrant wash of sultry colour which enhances and complements the natural lustrous colour of your lips, containing ingredients infused with natural nourishing extracts that ensure your lips stay soft, smooth and commanding all day long."

"Just so," said Daisy and sat back with a smile infused with natural nourishing extracts.

Rahul continued, "Applied, I suspect, with a number thirty-six precision lip brush, adding definition outward from the centre, with the edges filled in using a lip liner applied from the centre to the corners of your beautiful lips."

Daisy gave him a flat look, "Yes, shut up now Rahul. I'll see the chief Slag now."

Rahul turned and snapped his fingers. The chief Slag retrieval officer put down his crossword and left to retrieve the chief Slag. Like the rescue officer, his job title was very specific, leaving him with no duties for most of the time. Daisy briefly wondered if she should make bridge crew job titles a bit less specific.

Moments later, the chief Slag stood before Daisy. "So, Michigan Jones, how are your fellow refugees settling in?"

Jones stood blinking at her, his clothes and hair a total mess, his shirt open from navel to neck, exposing a firmly muscled bare chest that glistened with oil in the soft, complementary lighting of the bridge.

"Cor blimey," he grunted, eyes wide, "you must be the Queen!"

Daisy laughed regally. "No, no, you strange little beast, captain will do."

Jones coughed and twisted a cloth cap, which had suddenly appeared in his hands. "Well, your majest — uh, Captain, thank gods you came when you did. We had given up all hope, and the crew had no faith in me, guvnor, because of my total inability to think smart like what you do. And any man who'd been in a relationship with you and didn't know what he had would really regret letting you go, being as how smart, clever and fit he suddenly realises sadly too late that you are."

"Well, that's not for me to say. Although it's true."

"Your lips look bloody lush," Jones added, clearly overawed.

"Yes, yes, they do. Well now, settle in, we have a week or so until we arrive at Upsillion VII. It's a terraformed world, uninhabited but with infrastructure in place. You Slags can settle there and ruin the environment and then blame everyone else, like the poor workpersons you are. OK?"

Relief flooded over Jones's face. "Cor blimey, it's more than what we deserve and no mistake, what wiv our mindless alcoholism and fags and pickled invertebrates wot we luv for some reason."

He left the bridge in a furious twitch of bowing and scraping and cloth cap twisting.

#

Jones was having trouble walking. After he had stumbled for what seemed the thousandth time, he stopped and sighed. He looked down at his feet accusingly. "Really?" he demanded.

Walking in the absolute nothing in which he found himself was odd, to say the least. There were no reference points by which he could gauge progress, no sign that he was moving at all. It forced his brain to work overtime to try to make sense of things, and so it began to think consciously about the physical sequence of muscle movements that normally made up what it had commonly and unconsciously understood as the concept of walking. This had the unintended consequence of Jones continually tripping over his own feet. He sighed again. How the bloody hell can you forget how to walk?

Wait. His eyebrows shot up. Was that . . . something?

Peering into the distance, he could discern what looked like a collection of corrugated metal sheets leaning against each other in a vague pyramid form. They were lit by an intense, white light that almost obliterated any detail.

"OK legs," he said, "let's try this again, shall we."

Upon arrival at the something, Jones was disappointed to find that it was exactly what he had first imagined it to be — a collection of corrugated metal sheets leaning together to form a rough, brightly illuminated pyramid.

Then he spied something else beyond the pyramid. Oh, he thought, not one but two somethings. My, my.

On closer inspection the something else turned out to be an old couple: ancient, if their clothing was any guide. They both wore clothes in the style of ancient Earth's English Tudor period. They were seated, playing chess. Like the corrugated metal pyramid, they were lit with an almost blinding white light that washed away any colour and created harsh shadows on their craggy faces.

"Hello?" said Jones.

One of the couple, a man with the keen, red-ringed, welcoming eyes of a murderous psychopath, turned to look at Jones. He said nothing in response to Jones's greeting and instead turned back to his colleague, an old woman for whom the word 'wizened' seemed to have been specifically invented to describe.

"Did you see?" she asked of her companion.

"Why, did you?" said the psychopath.

"Hello? I'm right here," called Jones. "I mean, it's not like you could miss me. Aside from you two, I'm the only other bastard thing here. Oh, and the pyramid." He really had no truck for this sort of nonsense.

"But," continued the woman, "how do I know that what I think I see, is what you think you see?"

"Oh, good point," said Jones. "Let's try an empirical approach, shall we?" He marched up to the couple and grabbed the chessboard from the table, scattering the pieces in all directions. Then, bending first to one and then the other, firmly smacked each of them in the face with it. "Oh," he said, throwing the board over his shoulder. "But now how do you know that what I smacked you in the face with was what I smacked him in the face with? Huh, yes, I see, not so easy this talking bollocks stuff, is it." Jones shrugged and stomped off into the darkness. Pretentious bollocks really pissed him off.

Alone again in the darkness, the stunned couple looked at each other.

"Oh," said the psychopath.

"Bit fucking rude," said the old lady.

#

Smiert could not help but laugh.

She sat around a large table with her ship mates eating a well-deserved meal. The mood was celebratory. They had defeated the monster, escaped the cargo hold and, as for Jones and WindyMane, well, that had turned out better than expected.

She looked over at the couple, which was how they could now be described. They sat smiling and laughing with each other, WindyMane with her hoof protectively on her bulging midriff. She refused any offers of alcohol.

Daisy, Tongue, WindyMane and Jones all chattered happily, laughing at their recent exploits, the room positively awash with relief.

Smiert winced as a sudden, sharp pain shot through her chest. Indigestion, she thought. She had, after all, been eating like a giant, making up for the stresses and strains of the last few hours. Even so, she had been surprised at how hungry she was, gulping down whatever came her way. A corner of her mind noted that she particularly hankered for anything rich in protein.

"Ow!" The second stab of pain was much sharper than the first.

Daisy looked up. "You alright, Doctor?"

The chatter in the room dulled a bit, the others shooting curious glances in her direction.

"Yes, yes, is nothing," Smiert waved away their concerns.

The laughter and gay chatter resumed.

Another stab.

This time Smiert could not help but scream. She stood, her hand on her chest, coughing, trying to catch her breath. This time, the pain was off the scale.

All chatter in the room ceased.

Smiert screamed again.

The room stilled for a moment. Then everything seemed to happen at once.

Smiert found herself pinned to the table by the others.

"What's inside me!" she screamed. "What's inside me?"

"Hold her down, she might swallow her tongue!" someone said.

"That's not actually possible!" Smiert shouted.

"Isn't it?" said the voice.

"Quick, let me punch her." WindyMane's voice.

"No need, she's not choking."

"Quick, let me choke her."

"Shut up, WindyMane. Hold her down, she might injure herself."

"Why should she have all the fun?"

The pain in her chest intensified. "Please," Smiert shouted, "It . . . it's coming out of my chest!" Something deadly stirred within her, yearned and reached for release, burrowing its way closer and closer to the surface. She felt like her chest was going to explode. The pain seared outward, tearing toward the surface.

Smiert released a massive belch. All pain ceased.

The others recoiled in disgust.

"Jeebuzz, what the hell has she been eating?"

"That's revolting."

"I think I swallowed my tongue!"

Smiert sat up.

"Ah," she said, "Sorry. Just indigestion. My bad."

#

WindyMane gasped awake.

She was lying on a single bed in a cheap hotel room. A very cheap, sparsely furnished hotel room. The only illumination came from the single bare bulb hanging from a cord in the centre of the ceiling. The window was open, letting in the sounds of the night time traffic from the street below.

She didn't have a clue where she was or why. Still less did she know who she was.

Disorientated, she moved over to the window and glanced outside. The hotel, if that is what it was, was located on a busy street in what looked like a major city. Advertising videos streamed across the face of almost every building: they depicted happy Ululations with happy children happily consuming happy things. Answering a sudden urge to seek the familiar, WindyMane leaned dangerously out of the window, twisting around to look up into the sky.

Aha.

A large star-like object floated almost directly above. So, she was back on her homeworld, the Scents Globe, and the object shining above in the night sky was its twin planet, the Nonsense Sphere. Or maybe it was the other way around? Difficult to tell.

The Scents Globe and Nonsense Sphere, twin planets in stable orbit around the binary stars of the

Testiculon system, were home to the Zebroid Ululations.

Originally, so legend had it, the Zebroids of the Nonsense Sphere were entirely black and those of the Scents Globe entirely white. When developments in space travel enabled them to meet, the 'not like us' psychopathy of their evolution kicked in with a vengeance.

So began the War Without End.

The war lasted countless aeons until the coming of the one called Gavin Starmane.

Born to parents of both races, Gavin was the first of the stripy Zebroids. He preached of peace and tolerance and baking biscuits, which was something everybody felt was a good idea. Especially the stuff about biscuits, whatever they might be. And so they returned to their respective planets to give it a go. In honour of the Starmane, and to emulate their hero, they set out on a programme of mass interbreeding, which everyone agreed was a lot more fun than all that fighting stuff.

Thus, they renamed the 'War Without End' the 'War Without End Except For When It Ended And All the Sexy Stuff Started. And Biscuits, Of Which We Are Now Very Much In Favour'.

One day, so the legends said, he disappeared

without warning and though they grievously mourned his loss, Gavin Starmane was prophesied to return at a time of greatest Zebroid need. The Ululations eagerly awaited this second coming, hopeful that, whatever the trials and tribulations, it would conclude with the need for them all to get sexy again.

There would be parades and everyone would bake sexy biscuits.

WindyMane turned away from the window and examined the room. Its bare furniture told her nothing, but on the table rested a briefcase. Surely this could tell her who she was and why she was here? She quickly dialled the code on the combination lock. So, some memories remained to her.

Interesting.

After a brief pause to take a few deep, steadying breaths, she opened the case.

It contained a bewildering array of items: thick wads of notes in various currencies, dog-eared file folders, photographs, several passports and two lethal looking pistols.

Well, she considered, all pistols looked lethal. Being lethal was their job.

She inspected the passports. Each contained a photograph of her, which she confirmed with a quick glance in the room's dirty mirror, but each was in an unfamiliar name: 'SmellsSlightlyOfTurtles', 'DancesWithDifficulty', 'WhispersWithCheese'. All nondescript, traditional Ululation names that no one would afford a second glance. Hmm.

Suddenly her equine ears twitched. Several boot steps clumped up the hotel stairs and assembled themselves outside the door.

What the hell?

"Open the door!" came a voice from the other side.

"No, I'm not in," shouted WindyMane.

"Yes you are," said the voice.

Touché.

She was clearly faced with an opponent of considerable wit and mental dexterity. She had to think quickly.

"No, I'm not. Please leave a message after the tone. Beep."

There was a pause. "Oh, er, right, god I hate using these things, um, hello I'm Detective Sergeant —"

Another voice cut him off, "Oh get out of the way." The door rattled as a hoof pounded against it.

"Oi, you in there, open this door. I'm not going to say it twice!"

WindyMane waited in the silence that followed, wondering what in Starmane all this was about.

"Open this door!" demanded the voice.

"You said you weren't going to say it twice," said the first voice.

"What?"

"You said 'open this door, I'm not going to say it twice'. And then you said it again."

"Oh," said the second voice. "Good point." The door rattled again as the battering resumed.

"Open this door! Happy now?"

"Oh yes," said the first voice, "Yes, that's thrice, not twice."

"Hello? Are you in there?"

"No," WindyMane shouted back, "I already told you I'm not here."

"Well, that settles it," said the first voice, "we'll have to come back later."

The door burst open in a hail of splinters and other bits of door.

Two policemen rushed in. "Oh, you fibber," said the smaller of the two.

"What do you want?" said WindyMane, "And whatever you do, don't look in that briefcase on the table."

"I am arresting you on suspicion of being the

notorious international spy and assassin BlackWindow," said the larger officer.

At the sound of the name 'BlackWindow', WindyMane became still. "You can't arrest me," she said, her voice now even and emotionless.

"Oh, and who's going to stop me?" said the big one.

Thirty seconds later, WindyMane stood amidst the wreckage of what had once been a perfectly acceptable, if not cheap and nondescript hotel room.

And what had once been two conscious policemen with their arms and legs in the normal places.

JONES WAS STOMPING. In the absence of any other way to vent his anger, a bloody good stomp was all he had, and he was making the most of it.

Stomp, stomp, stomp.

Where the hell was he? Stomp.

How was he going to get out? Stomp.

Was he supposed to take this as some kind of metaphor for his subconscious? Stomp.

Jones hated metaphors. He liked things obvious and upfront. Ugh, and he really didn't want to think about subtext.

Stomp, stomp, stomp, stomp, stomp.

Jones liked to understand things, mostly so that he could avoid them. He didn't like it when meanings hid — how can you avoid something if it avoids telling you what it is? Poetry, for example. What does the poet mean here? What does the poet *mean*?! Maybe the poet should just state exactly what she means up front and save everyone a lot of bother. Enjoy watching the clouds pass on a summer's eve? Well, why not bloody well say that instead of dancing around what you mean like some sort of coked-up pretentious prog rock word wizard! What was the point of torturing language by forcing it into iambic pentameter when you could simply say "Is it just me, or does that cloud look like a massive cock?"

No, Jones had had enough of this place. He wanted out. Now.

Stomp, stomp, stomp, stomp, stomp, stomp, stomp.

As Jones rounded another of the corrugated metal pyramids, the third since his encounter with the pretentious old couple, he heard a harsh, sharp bark of a laugh. The sort of forced laugh a mid-level sales manager makes when the boss says something she thinks she ought to laugh at, like "Your husband is a surprisingly sensitive lover".

Jones stopped and looked down. A man sat cross-legged on the floor. Younger than the chess playing couple, but whereas they wore Tudor style clothing, this man wore something more like a Tarot influenced harlequin. Jones pursed his lips.

The man looked up. He had sharp, angular features. A bruise-like darkness that implied a dangerous lack of sleep encircled his eyes.

"Something funny?" asked Jones.

The deranged harlequin stood or, more accurately, unfolded himself into a standing position.

"Can you be more specific?" asked the harlequin, his pointed face seeming to cast accusations with barely suppressed hints of violence.

"OK. Who the hell are you supposed to be and what the hell are you laughing at?"

"Oh," said the harlequin, taken aback. "Yes, well, that is quite specific. That's not the sort of response I was looking for, I have to admit. Um, well, how can I answer? What, after all, is a cloud? Is it a face, a mountain, an animal?"

"Or is it a fist? No, this is a fist," Jones held up his right hand, "Or is it? Perhaps it's a cloud? Shall we find out by smacking you with it?"

"My, my, aren't we a seething ball of frustration? Well then, let's try this."

The countenance of the harlequin shifted and reformed. Jones found himself looking at his own reflection.

"Is that supposed to be me?" he demanded.

"I don't know, is it?"

"Right, bye then." Jones moved off to resume his stomping.

"Wait, wait, wait," the harlequin Jones followed the pissed off and impatient Jones, rushing to keep up. "Look, Jeebuzz, you're hard work. Why so angry?"

"Either point me in the direction of the exit or get out of my way."

"But this place is paradise, isn't it? Nothing to do, nothing to annoy me . . . I mean you . . . us."

"'Nothing' is an aspiration, it's an ambition. You have to work at achieving nothing. Fight for it. You want to get to the end of the day, look back and say, 'Yes, today I made no material difference to the universe. Today I achieved bugger all'. And the best way to achieve bugger all is by having a bloody good time. This is not a bloody good time."

"Ah, so we're a hedonist."

"*We* are nothing. *I* am a pisshead. A party were-wolf." Jones stopped walking and rounded on his doppelgänger. "Why advance medical science to the point where you can abuse your body as much as you like with no consequences if you then *don't* abuse your body and enjoy no consequences? It's madness. It's disrespecting the entire history of medical science. All those brave scientists who worked long, hard hours just so that I can get shit faced every night with no ill effects. That's not hedonism, it's respect."

"Ah, but those hard working scientists achieved the advances that enable you to behave in such a fashion. So there is a point to ambition and achievement."

"Oh, don't get me wrong. If other people want to go around achieving things, that's up to them. Each to their own, I say. Drink and let drink."

"But where would you be without their efforts? Where would you be if you were unable to abuse your body without consequences?"

"Dead of alcohol poisoning, probably."

Harlequin Jones sighed. "Why did you sign up to be XO of a starship?"

"This again? It's a position that looks like you are doing something, without you actually having to do anything. Everyone just assumes you are busy. Being XO means you get to tell other people what to do, and they sod off and do it and leave you alone."

"Ah. So all this stuff with monsters and 1960s purple sex gas is ruining all that. Trapped with the monster, you have to do things."

"The worst kinds of things. Dangerous things."

"So all you really want is to get out of here."

"Yes!"

"Oh. Well, I can tell you that."

"You? I thought you were a part of this whole . . . metaphor bollocks."

"Well, I am. I thought turning myself into you would freak you out but instead . . . I'm thinking like you. Bugger. I'm supposed to show you how totally vacuous and empty your life is, but now I really can't be arsed. Frankly, the sooner I don't exist, the better."

"Spoken like a true poet. So how do I get out?"

"Oh well, that's easy. WAKE UP!"

#

Smiert screamed.

Not an ordinary scream. Not the kind of scream you scream when stubbing your toe on a camou-flaged toe-stubbing brick left around by your unem-ployed inventor partner who has decided to make his fortune in the niche sector of 'creating things that don't exist for very good reasons, because people will think it's a quirky idea and they'll sell like hot sand-paper cakes, hot sandpaper cakes being another of my super brilliant inventions.' Not that kind of scream.

And not the kind of scream you scream when

opening your pants drawer and find it infested with slavering werewolves having a custard party.

No, this was the kind of scream you scream when you are giving birth and are really pissed off about it, because you don't recall having been pregnant in the first place.

Which was exactly the situation in which Doctor Smiert now found herself.

She had been in labour for some forty days and forty nights, which, as any mother will tell you, is the bare minimum for how long the process takes. This is in marked contrast to the process of actually getting pregnant in the first place, where forty seconds is generally considered the bare maximum. And that was the other annoying part about this situation — Smiert had absolutely no recall concerning the hot, sweaty, fumbling side of things.

She screamed again: not because of contraction pains this time, but just out of sheer bloody annoyance.

A nurse popped his head up from what was currently the business end of her.

"I can see the head, not long now," said Nurse Tongue cheerily.

"Tongue! What is going on? How did this happen? How am I here?"

"Well, the father of the child inserted his —"

"We were in mess, eating . . . no, before that . . . Jelloids . . . cargo bay . . . Kettlewick! Nyarghhhhhh-hhhhh!" Smiert screamed. This one was the kind of scream you scream when your genitals are ripped apart and pulled over your head. Or as the medical terminology would have it, 'childbirth'.

"And there we are!" shouted Nurse Tongue triumphantly.

Smiert flopped back onto the sweat-stained pillows, fatigue washing over her. "What, what is it?" she gasped.

"It's a bouncing baby saviour of the universe," Tongue beamed, handing the now swaddled bundle of baby messiah to Smiert. "Say hello."

Smiert looked down at her newborn. A small, stripy Michigan Jones squinted up at her.

"Why does my baby look like zebra?"

"What shall we name him?" asked Nurse Tongue brightly.

"Stalin," Smiert smiled up at him. "It was mother's name."

"I know," continued Tongue, "What about Gavin Starmane?"

"What? Gavin? No, this is not —"

"Yes," continued Tongue, "Gavin Starmane.

Excellent. Now would Daddy like to hold young Gavin?"

Gavin Starmane? Had she really given birth to the second coming of the Ululation messiah? The saviour of the universe? Well, that might explain the immaculate conception. Hang on — daddy?

Daddy stood next to the bed, all eight foot tall ebony killing machine of him. He extended his quivering jaw, saliva gushing over triple rows of razor teeth.

"I wish to cover him with my lumpy lubricant jelly," he hissed.

"Aw," Nurse Tongue rapidly blinked back tears as he fanned his face with open palms.

Realisation dawned on Smiert. Suddenly, she understood what her subconscious was trying to tell her. "Ah," she said, lying back.

"Now then," said Nurse Tongue, holding up a syringe. He tapped at the barrel.

"What is this?" frowned Smiert.

"Just a little something to help you WAKE UP!"

#

WindyMane, or 'BlackWindow' as she now thought of herself, surveyed her devastating handiwork, breathing heavily. By Gavin's mane, she was out of condition!

Even so, she was apparently still capable of taking out two armed detectives. Or, in this case, capable of taking out the arms of two detectives. She chuckled to herself as she stepped over the bodies. She had once taken out a six-armed detective on the shores of the Desiccated Sea, an ocean made of negative water that dehydrated anything with a hint of moisture. But that was easy — she had simply pushed him into the water and watched him wither into a juiceless husk.

She walked across to the mirror and adjusted her mane. Urgh, those mane braids would have to go. She smiled at her reflection. She had been wrong about the black leather catsuit. It suited her perfectly.

"All coming back to you, is it?" said a face in the mirror.

"Who are you?"

"Was. I *was* Plato. When I was alive. These days I'm a ghost of my former self." He laughed at his own joke — a dusty, arid, hollow sound. When Black-Window failed to respond, he harrumphed and dropped his smile. "Oh well, have it your own way. I am your emergency reboot apparition. In the event your cover is compromised, I am to reboot your original persona and put you in contact with the Stripy Council."

"I see. Well, you'd better get on with it then."

Plato's ghost harrumphed once more. "Yes. Hello, this is emergency reboot apparition calling the Stripy Council. I have a caller who wishes to place a reverse charge call. Do you accept the charges?" He listened to an inaudible voice for a moment. "Very well. Go ahead caller," he said to BlackWindow. His image disappeared from the mirror.

She inclined her head. The mirror blacked out, reflecting nothing. Three hooded Zebroid faces appeared from the blackness. The Stripy Council, directors of the Secret Herd, that most secret of secret organisations within the Ululation government. Of course. One of them leaned forward.

"Well, this is an unfortunate turn of events. Have your memories fully returned?"

"Well," she said, "I know my name is not Windy-Mane and I am not Poo-Pi-Doo to an idiot human. I also know," she briefly turned to look at the unconscious detectives, "that I am pretty tasty with my hooves."

"As you should be. You would not be much use as a deadly super-secret agent otherwise. This," he indicated the Ululation to his left, "is PrancesWith-Nickers, and this," he indicated the Zebroid on his right, "is ExpressesMilkInappropriately. I am NomDePlume. Not our real names, of course."

"Of course. So, I assume this is not really the Scents Globe and is instead some kind of hallucination caused by those two bum heads in the cargo bay?"

"Precisely," said PrancesWithNickers. "Your emergency apparition activated as soon as it detected they had taken over your mind. It had to assume your cover was blown and interceded to trigger your awakening. Your thoughts are no longer under the control of the, er, 'bum heads'."

"How much do you remember?" asked ExpressesMilkInappropriately.

"Do you remember your memory wipe?" asked PrancesWithNickers.

NomDePlume nudged his colleague. "If she could remember her memory wipe, it wouldn't have been much of a memory wipe, would it? Idiot."

"Why did I agree to that?" BlackWindow frowned. She did not like having gaps in her memory. Gaps were dangerous. Especially the ones between platforms and trains.

"The Stripy Council were suspicious and

wanted to know more about the events concerning the apparent arrival of the Herald of the Second Coming of Gavin Starmane. How could the herald be a human?" The Ululations to either side of NomDePlume spat with disgust. "Who is this 'Michigan Jones'?" Once more PrancesWithNickers and ExpressesMilkInappropriately hawked and spat. "So I drew up secret plans to find out." Again NomDePlume's colleagues spat their disgust. He gave them a flat look.

"Oh," said PrancesWithNickers.

"Sorry," said ExpressesMilkInappropriately, "got carried away, sorry."

"So you sent me deep undercover posing as a Poo-Pi-Doo biographer and historian. Such a cover would allow me to ask as many questions as I liked without drawing suspicion. Clever."

"It is clear that the two known as Tongue and Smiert are attempting to resurrect Gavin Starmane. BlackWindow, it is imperative that we learn the why and how of their plans. Do not tarry —"

"Do not!" PrancesWithNickers held up a hoof of warning.

"No tarrying!" ExpressesMilkInappropriately added, shaking his mane.

"Once you have learned all you can, you are to

kill Tongue and Smiert. Without prejudice. And one more thing."

"Yes?" said BlackWindow.

"WAKE UP!"

#

Captain Daisy Daryl stopped powering down the corridor, lifted her leg and examined the sole of her left shoe. Whatever she had just stepped in was disgusting and lumpy and smelled of unpleasantness.

It was definitely the type of thing you should avoid putting your foot in, and she probably would have if she had been able to see where she was going. But most of the corridor lights were out, and those that weren't just hung dangerously from the ceiling and flickered rapidly, doing their utmost to give everyone a migraine.

Neither puddles of this . . . stuff, nor poor lighting maintenance had any place on her once gleaming starship. She rubbed her boot on a nearby door frame, making "Euw" noises.

It had been one week since she had taken the Slags onto her ship.

One week.

In that time, things had gone to pot. Her ship no

longer gleamed; congealed in its own decay was more the mark.

Well, she would put up with this no more. They would soon pass a rocky planet with a couple of habitable moons. She would off-board the Slags there and get her ship back into some semblance of order. The admiral would be disgusted at the state of his flagship. And she couldn't say she blamed him.

No, she didn't blame the admiral. She blamed Michigan Jones. His lack of order, control and self-discipline had infected the ship and crew like a virus.

She continued on her way to the bridge, noting the crew members slouched in corners, smoking cigarettes or passed out in doorways. She would court-martial them all. Every single one of them.

She approached the door to the bridge. Instead of smoothly sliding open with a comforting 'swish' noise, it remained resolutely shut. She waited, tapping her foot.

Eventually, she gave in and stabbed at the manual control. The door opened an inch and then stopped, motors whirring in protest. Finally it slammed open, rusting metal screaming in protest like somebody dragging polystyrene fingers down a chalkboard.

Daisy took one step onto the bridge and halted,

coughing heavily as she breathed in the swirling smoke. What the hell had happened to the pristine air of the ship's nerve centre?

She waved a hand, trying to clear the smog before her face. "Jeebuzz, is something on fire?"

"Oh hi Daisy, come on in," Jones's voice sounded from somewhere inside the fog.

She entered her bridge. The tang of overpowering opiates and exotic herbs had replaced the smell of efficiency and order. Instead of applauding her, her bridge officers slouched around in various states of disrepair. She paused, awaiting the formal announcement of her presence. Instead, someone shouted, "Shut the bloody door".

Another one for the court-martial list.

Michigan Jones sprawled in her chair, a satisfied and faraway look on his face. He held a smoking something in his hand. "Hey, Daisy, what's new in captain land?"

"You are in my chair," she said, the words barely escaping her clenched teeth.

"I'm in *a* chair," he said, "Although, in a sense, aren't we all in the captain's chair?"

"No, in no sense are we all in the captain's chair. The captain should be in the captain's chair, but she isn't. Her chair is currently occupied by a vast slug and he needs to sod off."

Jones smiled dreamily, "Hey, why so uptight, lovely lady?" He held out the smoking thing to her. "Go on," he said, "You know you want to, why not relax, haven't you earned it?"

A whole barrage of logical and reasoned arguments sprang up in her mind, ready to organise themselves into coherent sentences and launch themselves in a very precise order at him. But then, she considered, he had a point.

She *had* earned the right to a little R&R . . . hadn't she?

Jones held out the narcotic again. "Go on," he said, "It would be so easy, all the cool officers are doing it."

She hardly heard the words. Daisy's attention was fixed on Jones's head. Where had those horns come from? That wasn't right, was it? She blinked and shook her head, marshalling her thoughts.

"XO," she called, "Status?"

Rahul Khan hauled himself up from the floor, his flabby man boobs swaying. His once pristine shirt was crumpled and spattered with various stains, his hair knotted and unkempt.

He belched loudly. "Michigan Jones is great. So

cool. Chilled," he said, and then collapsed backwards in a heap. The heap lay giggling to itself.

Daisy rounded on Jones. "This is your fault, you Slag!" she spat.

"Hey, I didn't force them. See, you're so uptight all the time. They just needed someone to show them how things should be."

"You just wait until the admiral hears about this. He'll have you shot out of a torpedo tube!"

"I have heard about this already." The admiral's voice, her father's voice, filled the bridge. Jones smiled and pointed at the main viewer. Daisy whirled around.

"Dad, uh, Admiral, I can explain. The Slags . . . distress call . . . the Biased Zone . . ."

"Yes, Silly Knickers, Jones has explained all this to me already."

"He did WHAT?" She threw an accusing glare at Jones.

"Yes, he put in a report an hour ago. I was a little disappointed that I had not already heard officially from you."

"We were too far away from a relay station. I have prepared my official report, it's ready to send —"

"No, don't worry, Mr Jones has brought me up to speed. I am most impressed."

"Oh, well, I know how you like things done Admiral —"

"The way you shot at the refugee ship by mistake."

"The way I did what by what?"

"Fortunately, the quick thinking Mr Jones saved the refugees by using lasers to deflect the torpedo with a glancing blow, placing it on a trajectory calculated to destroy the Glass battle cruisers that were threatening to destroy you after you mistakenly drifted into the Biased Zone. Excellent."

Daisy's brows knotted. "Whut?" was all her pent up fury could articulate.

"Yes. Very impressive. Prevented a war and saved your ship and crew. Not bad."

Daisy swung back to the slouching Jones. "Get. Off. My. Bridge."

"I can't," said Jones, smiling up at her.

"No indeed. He needs to stay on the bridge," said the admiral. "He impressed me so much, I have enlisted him. Say hello to your new EO."

"Dad, we've been through this. It's XO not EO and — wait, what?"

Jones leaned forward and offered the smoking

thing once more. "Go on," he said, "I'm on duty. You can relax."

Helplessly, Daisy turned back to the admiral. But her demand that he reverse his decision stuck in her throat as he took a long puff of a giant smoking thing, nodded and smiled blearily down at her from the main viewer.

Jones.

Jones was poison.

Jones was the devil.

Jones was everything wrong with everything in the universe.

Jones.

#

"Jones," said Daisy, sleepily.

Jones popped his head up from under the covers. "Sorry, yes, I was trying to find that other slice of pizza. Bloody thing's here somewhere," he said.

"What the hell have I done?"

"Well," said Rahul, sitting in an armchair across the room, "having given up all hope, you accepted and ingested massive amounts of narcotics and through a drug-addled haze suddenly found Executive Officer Jones amazingly attractive and invited him back to your cabin, whereupon you used your lips to —"

"Yes, yes, thank you, Exposition Officer. Wait, have you been sitting there all the time?"

"Yeah," said Jones, "we needed someone to hold the camera, remember?"

"Oh," said Daisy. For some reason, none of this alarmed her. When did she stop caring?

"Well anyway, Rahul," she said, "could you piss off now?"

He stood, sheepishly handed the recorder to Jones, and left the room.

Daisy regarded Jones. "It's all so easy for you, isn't it?" she said to his back as he put away the recorder.

"Easy? What is?" he murmured.

"Life. Everything. You're a complete and total freeloader and yet . . . people just fall over themselves to give you whatever you want. The rest of us, we have to work at stuff. If we want something, we have to earn it. But not you. Everything just falls into your lap."

He turned to look at her. He really was handsome, she thought. "Like you, you mean?" he smiled.

"Yes," she agreed, "But I'm not convinced that was a good idea."

"Want to go again? More data might lead to a re-evaluation of your conclusions."

Jones moved to embrace her, but she pushed him away. "No. One of us is supposed to be on the bridge at all times. We've been away too long already."

"Aw screw the bridge, the crew know what they're doing."

The red alert sounded.

"Red alert, red alert, there's a red alert and none of us know what we're doing!" came a panicked voice from the bridge. Daisy leapt from the bed and punched the communicator on her desk.

"Bridge. This is the captain. What's going on?"

"Captain," came Rahul's voice, "It appears we have been travelling in circles. We are back in the Biased Zone."

"What? How the hell did that happen?"

"No one's manning navigation."

"Get us the hell out of here!"

"We can't! Engines are out."

"At the risk of repeating myself, how the hell did that happen?"

"Essential maintenance has not been . . . maintained."

"Where the buggering flaps is the engineer?"

"He's set up a hippie commune with the navigation officer."

"Well, arrest him and get those bloody engines online."

"Too late, Captain — the governments of the Glass Half Full and the Glass Half Empty have formed an alliance and have declared all out war."

"What? On who?"

"On you, Captain."

Another voice filled her cabin. "Daisy Daryl, what have you done?!"

Daisy blinked and looked around for the source. "Dad?"

Standing behind her, partially obscured by shadows, was a tall cowled figure. The figure stepped into the light, raised his hands and threw back the hood to reveal the face beneath.

An Ululation stared down at her, its Zebroid face calm and relaxed.

"Hello Daisy," it said, "I am Gavin Starmane and you really must WAKE UP!"

Daisy, Jones, Smiert and WindyMane blinked and looked around as reality rudely resumed normal service.

"WAKE UP!" Derek's artificially amplified voice shouted again.

"We are, we're awake, we're awake," Daisy said, waving her arms like a disoriented drunk trying to ward off the alarm clock.

"How are we awake?" Jones staggered, "What even is awake? Who . . . where is my face? Do I have a face? What's a face?"

Doctor Smiert slapped him, hard.

"That is face," she said.

"Jeebuzz! You could just have pointed!"

She slapped him again.

"Ow! What the hell!?"

"Did you feel that?"

"Yes, I felt it, you maniac!"

"Ah. Just checking I am no longer hallucinating. No, still awake. Is good."

"If that's all you wanted, I could just have pinched you."

"No, I would take your genitals."

"Alright, alright, let's focus shall we?" said Daisy, her wits reassembling themselves into a semblance of order.

They looked around. Derek, the misfit Emergency Klaxon, stood holding the severed heads of the Ululation medics formerly known as Balms and Unguents, latterly known as bum heads.

"Wow, nice work," said WindyMane. Smiert gave her a sharp look.

Daisy addressed the Klaxon. "Where is Kettlewick?"

Derek shrugged.

"He got away, good boy," said Smiert.

"Good boy?" queried Daisy, eyebrow raised.

Smiert's eyes widened. "No, I mean 'Good. Boy, that is good, he not here anymore'. My Galactix," she rolled her eyes, "What am I similar to? No. Like. What am I like?"

Daisy shook herself. Right, time to take control of

the situation and make this ship run more like a USS Fabulous and less like a bunch of Slags.

"Bridge, what's the ship's status?" Jones's voice echoed her own. She shot him a surprised glance. He shrugged.

"We'll be arriving at Telescopium in a few minutes," said Steve, "other than that, whatever passes for normal around here."

"Captain, is everything alright down there? We lost contact." Tongue's voice.

"Yes, Mr Tongue. We had a bit of a problem but all sorted now, we'll get back to you with next steps."

"Let me know as soon as we arrive at the black hole, cargo bay out," added Jones, annoyingly.

Daisy frowned. The words 'commanding', 'efficient' and 'Jones' did not go together. Could he still be under Kettlewick's control? But how if the telepaths were dead?

"Well," said Jones, turning to Daisy, 'Looks like we dodged a bullet there — OW!"

"Oh, sorry!" Mortified, Daisy reached out to touch the spot on Jones's face where she had slapped him.

Jones just crossed his arms and glared at her, sucking in his cheeks, eyes wide in an angry, silent stare. She didn't blame him.

"Sorry," she said again, "Wasn't thinking, I just .. . I thought you might still be hallucinating, you know, suffering delusions that you're a proper XO, no, look, sorry."

"So what happened to these two?" WindyMane kicked absently at one of the dead Ululations.

Smiert nodded towards the headless corpses. "I won't know for sure until I perform thorough autopsy. Maybe they strangled? Drowned? Perhaps they stabbed? You sure they dead? Have you checked for pulse?"

"I meant," said WindyMane, "what turned them from fine, upstanding Ululation medics into mind controlling bum heads?"

Was that a hint of danger in the Ululation Poo-Pi-Doo's voice? She seemed a bit more steely than usual. Daisy gave a mental shrug; it seemed they were all a bit shaken by their recent experiences.

Smiert waved a dismissive hand. "Exposure to Purple Sex Gas. Who cares?"

Daisy drew a deep breath. "Time for that later. We're minutes away from a black hole; let's get down to the computer core, reboot and get the hell out of here."

STEVE CHECKED THE TIME AGAIN.

Fifteen minutes until they reached the black hole. He ran through the plan for what seemed like the hundredth time. Arrive at the black hole; transfer and run all ship operations from his face; wait for the reboot to finish; transfer ship functions back to the computer; get crew out of the cargo bay; execute a slingshot around the black hole; deliver PSG to New Amsterdam; upgrade computer with the 'borrowed' files; get shit-faced; sleep.

All seemed straightforward. So why was he feeling so antsy?

He glanced over at Mic Vol. Yes. That was why.

He walked over to the communications officer. He didn't want the weird bastard floating over to him again. Difficult to have a proper conversation when the other person is floating.

"So, Mic," he said, by way of an opening, "do you wear that encounter suit all the time?"

Mic, or rather the suit, turned towards him. "Only in these dimensions." The suit turned back to his console.

"Ah," said Steve, briefly mourning the death of the conversation. "So, Mic," he tried again, "black hole of Telescopium, eh? Have your people ever visited it?"

"Visited? Not as you would understand the word, no."

"So you've never been there?"

"Please, let me finish. Not as you would understand the word no, but as you would understand the word, yes."

Steve's brain did some grammatical gymnastics. "So . . . you have been there?"

"Do you understand the word 'yes'?"

"Yes."

"Ah. Well, then yes, my people have been there."

"So there's nothing to worry about with this black hole? Perfectly ordinary black hole."

Mic slightly inclined his suit. "Why did you

choose this particular black hole? Just random, was it?"

"Well, not random no, I checked the star charts, and it was the closest, so . . ."

"I see."

"It was. I checked. The closest black hole to us is in the constellation of Telescopium."

"Of course. Telescopium. My people know it by a different name."

"What do they call it?"

Mic paused for a moment. "How to say . . . do you have a single word that describes the concept of blood-curdling terror and not being good at sports?"

"Not really. I suppose 'Phys Ed teacher' would be the nearest."

"Ah. Well, in our tongue the word is 'Aieeeeeeeeee!!!', not to be confused with the similar sounding but completely different word 'Aieeeeieeeee!', which means 'to squash one's genitals in a sitting accident'."

"Oh. I didn't know your people have genitals."

"We only wear them on formal occasions."

Steve let that comment go and pressed on. "So 'Aieeeeeeeeee!!!' that probably sounds worse than it is, right? I mean, our visit to this black hole isn't going to end in blood curdling terror or death or anything?"

"Death? I cannot see what a creamy yellow liquid made of milk solids and starch has to do with the black hole of Aieeeeeeeeee!!!"

"Creamy . . . Mic, how do your people perceive death?"

"In the same way your people perceive custard."

"What?"

"They are much the same if you think about it."

Steve thought about it. They were not the same. He said so.

"Precisely," said Mic, as if that clarified everything.

"Look, Mic, I just want to be sure. Is our visit to Aieeeeeeeeee!!! going to result in . . . custard or death or squashed testicles or anything?"

Mic paused. "Yes, all of those things."

"Oh Jeebuzz, I knew it!"

"Or perhaps only some of those things. Or none. It is difficult to tell. My people tend to avoid that particular location."

"Why?"

Mic considered. "It is like a . . . now what do you people call that subatomic particle . . . ah yes, it is like a strange quark."

"In what way?"

"It is strange."

Steve resisted the urge to punch his companion. Conversations with Mic were like having your brain put in a blender. "Strange quarks, yes, I see."

"No you don't."

"No, I don't. What the hell have subatomic particles got to do with the Telescopium black hole?"

"Hmm. Well, a strange quark is a *type* of quark, yes? Like a 'charm' quark or an 'up' quark. The problem is not the black hole *per se*, it's . . . the type of gravity it is composed of."

"Type of gravity? Gravity's just gravity. Isn't it?"

"No. There are different types of gravity. Just as there are different types of quark. And like quarks, some of them are strange."

Someone had just turned the blender up to full power and what remained of Steve's brain completed its transition into mush. "Mic, what are you talking about? And please, explain it like you're talking to someone with plankton for a brain."

"Different types of gravity attract different things. Have you ever wondered why you put bathroom furniture in the bathroom?"

"No."

"It's because that's where bathroom furniture wants to go. It is attracted to the part of the house where bathroom gravity is strongest, so all bathroomy things end up there. Kitchen gravity attracts kitchenware. In much the same way, social media attracts racists and bigots. Or, as you call them, social justice warriors."

"Wait, what? There's racist gravity now?"

"Yes."

"Right. OK, fine," said Steve. It was neither OK nor fine, but he let it pass. "So what type of gravity is this black hole made from?"

Mic inclined his suit, considering.

"Limerent," he said.

#

"So we're all agreed then," said Daisy.

"No," said Jones.

"Yes," said Smiert.

"Define 'agreed'," said WindyMane.

Great. They had reconvened in the operations room, and Daisy was trying to run a briefing on next steps. The way it should have gone is: Daisy explained the plan and they all agreed. Except, of course, it hadn't gone that way at all.

"Let's just have a quick recap," said Jones. "First, Kettlewick tried to suffocate us; then he tried to stab us all up; then when that failed, he got his bum heads to fry our brains. Now I don't have much by way of emotional intelligence or social skills or socially emotional touchy-feely nonsense, but I'm beginning to think he doesn't like us. Any minute now we'll get a postcard delivered saying 'Having a lovely vacation, wish you were dead'."

WindyMane tapped her hooves together thoughtfully. "Interesting that he has not sucked the oxygen from the whole cargo bay."

"So? Just means he prefers the personal touch."

"Or," WindyMane shot Jones a withering look, "it means he needs oxygen too."

Daisy's brows knitted. The Ululation seemed a lot more . . . intense since they had snapped out of their telepathic nightmares. She shook herself. This was no time for paranoia. Tuesdays. Tuesdays were the time for paranoia. Jones was speaking again.

"Great. So, before we do anything else, let's trap the bastard in an airlock and shoot him into space. No oxygen. Perfect."

"No!"

The room fell silent.

Well, this was new. The doctor was not usually squeamish. Psychotic, yes. Squeamish, definitely not. Daisy wondered what kind of personal hell the telepaths had subjected her to. "Something on your mind Doctor?"

"We can't kill it. Is new life form."

"Fine," said Jones. "Let's turn it into a new dead form."

"Why eject it? We could just trap in airlock."

WindyMane inclined her head. "That thing has fascinated you ever since it first appeared."

"Of course. I am doctor," said Smiert.

"Questionable," said WindyMane, "But even so, in our current situation being fascinated by Mr Kettlewick's promotion from chief engineer to murder tank is a bit like falling off a cliff and being fascinated by the natural beauty of the jagged rocks hurtling towards you."

"Listen," said Jones. "Waiting for me in my cabin, I have a keg, an entire keg, mind you, of Big Papa's Golden Papa Secretions. The only thing between me and the delicious flavours of Big Papa's Secretions is that bloody monster. I say we blow it out the airlock. The sooner we get rid of it, the sooner we end all this nonsense. I have tremendous amounts of bugger all I should be getting on with."

"Nice bit of prioritisation there, XO," said Daisy. "But we're out of time. If we don't reboot the computer when we arrive at Telescopium, we'll miss our chance."

"Daisy, this is a kill or be-stabbed-to-death-in-a-killing-stab-death-frenzy situation. So far, he's taken three shots at us. We need to deal with him before we reboot because sometime soon our luck is going to run out, and he's going to orphan my keg — why is no one thinking of my Big Papa Secretions?"

"Did you notice his back?" asked Smiert.

"Nope, too busy noticing its many, very sharp teeth and drooling saliva," said Jones.

"Go on," said WindyMane pointedly.

"When Jones let off lucky grenade, it was injured. Now, is not."

"Huh," mused WindyMane. "So it must have remarkable regenerative powers."

"Yes," said Jones, "But we don't. That's the point."

"The point is," added Smiert, "the medical advances we could make if we understood how it regenerate so fast."

Jones nodded. "Oh yes, the medical advances. And then there are the fantastic advances in the field of forensics. They'll have to develop new murder scene investigation techniques just so they can figure out which of our body parts belongs to which of our bodies. I say we blow it out the airlock before we do anything else."

"No," said Daisy. "Our priority is the computer."

"Well, you would say that," said WindyMane.

The room fell silent once more.

"Explain?" said Daisy, wielding the word in the same way one might smash the bottom off a glass bottle and wield it in someone's face.

"I agree with Jones; first we blow it out the airlock and then we can get to the core. There's no point being squeamish about it. Just think of it as finishing what you started."

Finishing what you . . .

A wave of boiling heat flushed over Daisy's body.

Finishing what you . . .

Her balled fists pounded against her thighs as she wrestled to contain her rising anger. *Steady Daisy, you are the captain. You must remain cool and — no, fuck it.*

"Now you listen to me, you stripy bitch!" Daisy advanced on WindyMane, only to find her way blocked by Jones.

"Like you said, we don't have time —"

"Spoilsport," muttered Smiert.

Daisy silently glared at Jones, breathing hard.

"Compromise," he said. "We head for the

computer core. The Klaxons go in the opposite direction, making as much noise as they can. Draw Kettlewick's attention so he doesn't take another pot shot at us. They trap him in the airlock. If it looks like he's going to break out, shoot the bastard off into space. If not, fine, the doctor gets her specimen. Agreed?"

His words gradually penetrated the furious fog clouding Daisy's mind. Fortunately, this furious fog was not like the Furious Fogs that roiled around the terminator zone of the tidally locked planet Furion VII. Nothing penetrated those, especially not the reasoned argument that if they were to stop being furious for a moment, they might stop roiling and be able to coalesce into solid forms, the lack of which was what made them so roilingly furious in the first place. No, hers was a furious fog that could be penetrated. Had Jones just proposed a sensible plan?

The conversation stopped as the group looked at each other, waiting for someone to hate on the idea.

Daisy opened her mouth, but before she could speak, Jones raised a hand. "And no," he said, "we can't put WindyMane in the airlock too."

She pouted, shoulders drooping. "Fine," she said. "Let's get on with it."

Smiert had considered wearing latex gloves for the delicate task ahead, but decided against. For this to work, she needed direct contact with the subject.

Her beloved Spongiform Jelloid project, not to mention the job for which Miasma employed her, required Spartan determination and, occasionally, extreme measures. Or even, like now, really gross and disgusting measures.

She took a deep breath and inserted her hand into the exposed brain of the dead Ululation medic, Balms. She had often wondered how it would feel to be a vet inserting an arm up the backside of a cow. Now she had a pretty good idea.

Come on Doctor, focus.

Smiert activated her bio-ware implants. She

knew exactly what she was looking for. Over the years she had examined, or rather, dissected, several telepathic brains. All of them dead, of course — for some reason live telepaths ran away screaming whenever she walked in the room. She reached out with her implant sensors, questing for a particular psychic resonance.

She could not know for certain if Balms and Unguents had been telepaths, but they had possessed powerful psionic capabilities. Those usually went hand in hand, or rather mind in mind, with telepathy.

Only one way to find out.

Ah yes! There they were, the neural cells marking out a telepathic cluster.

Upon contact, her head spun with a peculiar vertigo as her consciousness lifted from the confines of her skull. It was a curious sensation, similar to weightlessness. She imagined this might be how a leaf would feel as it floated on the breeze.

Come on Smiert, she chided herself. *Get a grip, focus.*

She looked down at herself kneeling on the cargo bay floor, one hand holding a decapitated Ululation head, the other fisting its dead brain.

Not a good look, it had to be said.

She expanded her awareness outward, questing for a psychic resonance that matched Tongue. Quite how she did this, she was not sure, but she could not afford the time for a detailed analysis.

There. On the bridge.

Three orbs of varying brightness, one of them dominating the others by degrees of magnitude. This one did not feel like Tongue. The dim one? No, that, she felt sure, was Steve.

She focused on the middle orb. Yes. Without knowing how she knew, she was suddenly in no doubt that this was Tongue. So the brightest orb must be Mic?

Interesting.

She released herself towards the middle orb. Huh. It was a bit like pushing off from the side of a swimming pool: a single push, and she drifted in the desired direction. And so she would have continued had something not snatched at her awareness.

Instead of a graceful glide towards Tongue, her awareness suddenly veered off towards the brightest orb.

She tried to stop, but it was impossible. She was helpless, captured by the psychic gravity of the shimmering orb, rushing towards it.

Then, just as she felt sure she was going to crash

into it, whatever that meant in this state of being, it, Mic . . . noticed her.

Impossibly, he snared her consciousness as she hurtled towards him, spun and threw her at Tongue.

And then Smiert was looking at the bridge through Tongue's eyes.

"How did you do that?" she demanded of Mic, in Tongue's husky man-voice.

Steve looked up. "Is he being odd? Don't worry, he does that sometimes. Best ignore it," he said. He shrugged and returned his attention to the monitors.

Mic Vol inclined his body. "I sensed that was your intended destination. Was I incorrect?"

Tongue/Smiert excused him/herself from the bridge. In the corridor, he/she stopped.

"Get the hell out of my mind right now!" demanded Tongue. "No, first, tell me why you are in my mind. No, how? Any of that, tell me any of that. Now."

"Tongue listen, I must —"

"Get out of my head!"

"Right. You ask for this." Smiert/Tongue turned to the bulkhead and head-butted it.

"Ow, Jeebuzz, what the f —"

"Now listen. I do not know how long I have. Is important, yes?"

"Smiert, I'm warning you, if you — what are you doing?"

Smiert balled Tongue's fist. "Listen, or I punch you many times in testicles, yes?"

Tongue/Smiert gulped. "You have my attention."

"The sex gas, it changed Balms and Unguents into telepathic bum heads. But they dead now. I use their brains to communicate with you."

"How? No, don't answer that."

Smiert ignored him and flashed an image of what she was currently doing into Tongue's mind. After all, a misery shared . . .

"Oh Jeebuzz, you're disgusting! What the hell is wrong with using the intercom?"

"Too dangerous, could be intercepted. Listen — the Kettlewick monster has regenerative properties."

"And that's worth being elbow deep in brains, why?"

"Miasma wants an adult Starmane and they want him now. But I can't do that because speed growing biological tissue causes fatal damage. But if I can isolate the regenerative proteins in the monster . . ." It was this idea that Smiert's subconscious had been trying to communicate to her during her dream state.

"Of course — any damage caused by accelerated

growth will just repair itself. Understood. What do you want me to do?"

Smiert flashed images of her plan into Tongue's head.

"Are you sure that's wise?" said Tongue.

"You have better idea?"

Tongue thought for a moment. "No, fine. But we still need that fertilised egg. Get WindyMane and Jones into the computer core chamber. Then lock them in."

"Why?"

"The PSG canister I gave you. Once they've started the reboot, I want you to feed that into their air supply. We have an interspecies conception to bring about and I don't think gin will do the trick. We may not get another chance."

"How do I get them into the chamber? Our glorious captain will want to —"

Suddenly, Tongue was alone in his own mind again. Or was he?

"Smiert?" He remained still for a moment, questing in his thoughts until he was sure she was gone.

Had Smiert been able to read his mind? Was his mission compromised? No way to tell. Oh well, he'd just have to play it by ear and hope for the best. He moved off down the corridor.

He had work to do.

#

Back on the bridge, Steve watched the kaleidoscope of multi-coloured pyrotechnics on the main viewscreen as the ship exited the wormhole and re-entered normal space.

In the distance, a safe distance it relieved him to note, was the black hole; a spherical object of utter blackness squatting against the relatively lesser blackness of space.

He gulped, his mouth suddenly dry. He had been so confident about his plan, but that confidence had now fled, leaving behind a handwritten note that read 'ha ha, fooled you!'.

Mic Vol hadn't been reassuring. Despite his trying to elicit more information from his pan-dimensional friend, the answers just left Steve even more confused. One more go.

"Mic?"

There was no response. Mic sat staring into space.

"Mic."

Still nothing. Steve sauntered over to the comms station. "Mic!" he said, somewhat louder.

Mic jerked back, the arms of his encounter suit flailing.

"Whoa, whoa there fellah, didn't mean to startle you."

"Ah. I remember you. Barbara, is it not?"

"What? No, it's me, Steve."

"Steve?" Mic inclined the head segment of his encounter suit. "No, I am not Steve. We are aboard the Marie Celeste, yes?"

"Space Scrap 17."

"Oh yes!" Mic stood up urgently. "Yes, that is still happening. Yes, good, I am back in phase. Yes, hello? Yes?"

"Were you dreaming?"

"Dreaming . . . I suppose you could call it that. But," he made that weird shoulder shrugging motion that Steve always thought of as his equivalent of laughing, "Not one of those scary dreams where you can't move your eyebrows."

"What's scary about not moving your eyebrows?"

Mic inclined his suit, "Dirty bitch."

There was no answer to that. Once again, the conversation had derailed.

"Did you want something, Steve?"

"What? Oh, er, yes. Why 'Mic Vol'?" This was not what he wanted to ask, but could not bring himself to come straight to the point. Now that they had arrived at the black hole, he wasn't sure he wanted to hear the answers.

Mic sat up. Which was an odd move, because he was actually standing. "Why do I exist, you mean? Now, that is the first sensible question you have asked me. Also, a question vital to the future of —"

"No, I meant why did you choose the name 'Mic Vol'? Why not use your real name?"

For a long, uncomfortable moment, Mic stared at Steve. Then he visibly deflated, which was no mean feat given the encounter suit.

"So close," he muttered before drawing himself up once more. "My people," he said aloud, "do not have names so much as . . . vague suspicions."

"Wait a minute," Steve interjected. "Rewind a bit. What do you mean 'so close'?"

"So when I enlisted aboard the ship as communications officer I took my 'name', as you call it, from the first thing I saw on my board. Mic Vol seemed the most like a name."

Steve let it go. The communications officer was the one person on the ship incapable of communicating. Any question seemed to open up a whole warren of rabbit holes down which one could get lost, go insane, and eat one's own feet. No, he decided, best be direct. Stick to one rabbit hole and hope to keep at least one of his feet.

"So you were saying there are different types of gravity?"

"Yes."

"And this one is made of limerent gravity?"

Mic rocked back slightly and then inclined the top part of his encounter suit. He thought a bit.

"Yes."

Steve checked the definition of 'limerent' once more via his face tattoo's bacterial computers.

"How can gravity be limerent?"

"In this case, dangerously."

"OK, listen to me Mic and try, please try, to give me a straight answer. Is that black hole dangerous to this ship? Do I need to move us away?"

Mic thought for a moment. "Well, it will be perfectly safe unless someone causes an irresponsibly high wave of psychic resonance in the area."

"Right. No irresponsibly high waves of psychic resonance. Check."

"It will be perfectly safe unless someone causes an irresponsibly high wave of psychic resonance in the area. Like Doctor Smiert did just now when she flew onto the bridge."

So much for straight answers. "Mic, Doctor Smiert hasn't been on the bridge. She's trapped in the cargo bay."

"She is now."

"OK, sod this. I'm getting us out of here." Steve rushed back to his console.

He froze mid-step as a high-pitched voice broke into the usual background noise of the bridge. "Well, hello there." No, not just a high-pitched voice, a high-pitched voice with a slight reverb.

Steve looked around, trying to locate the source. Nothing. "Er, hello?"

The disembodied voice chuckled. "Don't sound so worried. I'm not going to hurt you. Much."

Smiert gasped like she was coming up for breath. She sat back on the cold metal floor of the cargo bay, panting.

"Doctor, are you alright?" Jones stood looking down at her.

"Jones," she gasped between breaths, "what year is it? Who is president?" She regarded the bodies and mashed brains of Balms and Unguents, momentarily confused.

"What are you rambling about? You've only been down here for ten minutes. Are you alright?"

"Yes, yes," she waved away his concern before realising her waving arm was covered in the lumpy grey remnants of Balm's brain. "I, uh, I just came down to . . ."

"Yes, I can see. Well," sniffed Jones, "we all have our hobbies, I suppose."

"I do not fist telepath brains for hobby. I was trying to use telepathic nerve clusters in brain to see if I could contact monster. Convince it we were away from computer core."

"Ah, did it work?"

"Of course not. For that, I would need military grade bio-ware implants . . . which I forgot I do not have." She gave a strangled laugh. Damn, she was disoriented. "Of course I don't. That would be mad and very suspicious."

"Whatever, look can you use one of these?" He held up a bulky device.

"What is it?"

"Tracking device we found in the cupboard. We wondered if you could calibrate it to locate the monster's bio-signature."

A tracking device? Smiert smiled inwardly. Very useful, very useful indeed. "Huh," she said aloud. "Very good. I will try." She stood and dusted down her lab coat.

"Right, well, come on then. We've got a computer to reboot."

#

The team that trudged along the darkened corridors was far from being a merry band of colleagues.

The air of gloom was not helped by the layers of grime and dirt that seemingly pervaded every surface. All bonhomie, such as it was, had evaporated. Deep shadows exaggerated the taut faces and furrowed brows, expanding and contracting across their faces as they marched grimly beneath the red overhead emergency lighting.

Initially, Daisy had blamed the sudden change in group dynamics on the reality-bending mind trip that Balms and Unguents had laid on them all. Things hadn't quite been the same since then. WindyMane, for example. Where once she had been a naïve and happy horsey — zebra, Daisy corrected herself — now she was cold and acid. Even the way she carried herself had changed: she moved less like a skippy, happy-slappy digital marketing content provider, and more like a precise, economical, ruthless killer who wasted no energy in unnecessary movement. Daisy raised her eyebrows. Ruthless killer? Now, where had that thought come from? And where WindyMane had once ignored Smiert, now Daisy repeatedly caught her glaring at the doctor with what looked like a wild hatred in her eyes. If a gaze could stab someone brutally to death,

Smiert would now be in tiny pieces scattered all over the corridor. And then there was the doctor herself.

Smiert seemed to be infatuated by the monster. Was it possible to get the hots for a slavering eight-foot tall killing machine? Even for Smiert, that was weird.

Jones had lost some of his 'devil may care, but then the devil would because he's just an annoying bastard out to make a point' attitude and smartened up his act. Now he seemed purposeful and focused, words that would not normally be associated with him. But who could blame him? Daisy had screwed this whole situation from the get-go. Could anyone blame him for deciding he, as XO, needed to take control, grab the bull by the horns? If someone like Jones had decided the situation was now so dire that even he could do a better job, then she must have really screwed up.

WindyMane had said it. It was Daisy who had allowed the consignment of PSG aboard the ship; Daisy who had insisted on stowing the cargo; Daisy who had lost control of the cargo loader and punctured a container; it was Daisy who was single-handedly responsible for causing the chief engineer to morph into a new, murderous life form with the single political aim of meeting new life and civilisations and then stabbing them all with primary and secondary talons. WindyMane was right, Daisy may as well finish him off. At least she would have brought one thing to a successful conclusion.

In short, Captain Daisy Daryl had to face facts: she was, without a shadow of a doubt, the worst captain ever to have commanded a starship. The harder she tried to prove to everyone that she had the chops, the more she proved the opposite. And now her rubbish XO had had enough and was angling for the top job, a job her father would no doubt hand him on a silver platter once all this was over.

If they survived.

She frowned at the thought.

No dammit, this was not how things were going to play out. She would not stand by and let everyone point and laugh and write her off. Bollocks to her father, bollocks to the crew, and especially bollocks to her newly ambitious XO, the bollocks of whom she would cut off and wear as earrings rather than let him swoop in and save the day.

She'd show them, she'd show them all!

Captain Daisy Daryl would prove to them she was worthy of the title and then, when she had rescued the ship and saved the lives of everyone on New Amsterdam, she would resign and sashay off into the distance, leaving an insulting note and a middle finger to boot.

The group rounded a corner in the corridor and came to a halt.

Daisy opened her mouth to speak.

"We're here," Jones announced.

She closed her mouth again.

Yes, she thought, she could do with a new pair of earrings.

#

"Bit of a let down really, isn't it?" said Jones, surveying the computer core antechamber.

"What were you expecting?" asked WindyMane, as she moved cautiously into the room.

"I dunno. Flashing lights, whirring computer tape decks, buttons, levers? You know, proper computery stuff. The unmistakable odour of concentrated geek lingering in the air, perhaps? Not . . . well a tube that looks like a one person deep-diving submarine." Jones indicted the featureless tube with his thumb.

"And snarky signage," said Smiert, reading a large magnetic sign attached to the bulkhead.

Jones joined her. '*Authorised personnel only,*' it

read. '*Only two people in the core at any one time.*

Or one enormous person.

Or one sort of large person and one tiny person.

Or no more than six octillion particles of gas-based entities.

And don't get on to HR about these signs being size-ist or size shaming or any of that bullshit — the core is compact with many dangerous buttons that should not be pressed.

Every ship has many dangerous buttons that should not be pressed.

We keep them all here, safely out of everyone's way, so that they stay unpressed, and there is only so much room in this chamber. Last thing we want is many dangerous buttons accidentally pressed by too many buttocks.

Don't believe us? Think we've got nothing better to do than get these signs printed and put up? Fine, go on, try to fit three average-sized people in there at the same time. Go on, we dare you. See what happens.

No?

Didn't think so.'

"I wonder how many people can get in there at any one time," said Smiert, her voice dripping sarcasm. She returned her attention to the tracking device.

Jones peered over her shoulder. "How are they getting on?"

"The Emergency Klaxons are making a lot of noise giving maintenance corridor 7-G a good vacuuming."

"And Kettlewick?"

"Moving towards them. Slowly."

"Good," said Daisy, "something is going right at least."

"Right, come on then," said Jones, "the sooner we get this basket case of a computer rebooted, the sooner we can all get out of here." He moved towards the door.

"Wait, where are you going Captain?" said Smiert.

Daisy halted mid-step. "Into the computer core. We'll need my command codes to authorise the reboot."

"My codes will do," said Jones.

"But it takes dual command keys. We have to turn them at the same time."

"Fine, WindyMane can go in," said Smiert. WindyMane stared daggers at her.

"The keys are DNA coded," said Daisy.

"Imprint WindyMane's DNA on it," said Jones.

"Why should WindyMane go in?" said Daisy,

her voice an octave or two higher than usual. Well, thought Jones, at least she hadn't reached shrill yet.

"Yes, why WindyMane? I'd like to hear the good doctor's reason for that too," said WindyMane, crossing her arms.

Jones clenched his jaw. This was getting ridiculous. "Bloody hell, fine. Smiert, you come with me. Captain, give her the key and authorise her DNA imprint," Jones waved her forward.

"Um, no, I must monitor the progress of the Klaxons. Also, I guard perimeter."

"Guard the perimeter?"

"Yes. Guard perimeter. Perimeters always need guarding. If you not careful, perimeter get up and move somewhere else and then you are not guarding perimeter at all. Is nuisance, should build self guarding perimeters but no, so I go to perimeter. Guard."

"What are you talking about, you mad bint? Actually, no, forget it. Perimeter, fine, whatever," said Jones. At least if she were somewhere else, he wouldn't have to listen to her nonsense.

"Now wait a minute," Daisy stepped forward. "I am still captain of this ship," she said, shooting Jones a pointed look, "and as such, this is my responsibility. I'm going in."

"But is menial task. Any idiot can turn key. WindyMane is ideal for idiot task." WindyMane did not reply to Smiert's remark, instead just smiled sweetly.

"It is my duty to safeguard this ship and —"

"And it is my duty to safeguard the captain," said Jones, "So that the captain can safeguard the ship. I'm sorry Daisy — Captain — I'm pulling XO command override."

"That only allows you to purchase extra coffee from the canteen," pointed out Daisy.

"And discounted quantities of Big Papa's Golden Papa Secretions from the bar, that's not to be sniffed at," added Jones. "And I would very much like to exercise that command override. In the bar. So, can we get this over with, please?"

Why the hell was she being so awkward? What did it matter who went into the core? All he wanted to do was get this bloody computer rebooted, get out of the cargo bay, not be eaten by a monster and get back to his normal life of caring about squat and doing bugger all. If that meant he had to square his jaw for a couple of hours, so be it. He just wanted to get on with it.

"Why not me and the captain?" WindyMane pointedly asked, her eyes shooting daggers at Smiert.

"Look, enough. Captain, in there we'll be isolated, and I'd feel a lot safer with a grownup on guard, which means you. Anything goes wrong, someone will have to make the big decisions. I'll go in with WindyMane. Smiert you go and guard the perimeter and make sure it doesn't . . . wander off. OK? We'll be in and out like a shot."

They all stared at Daisy. She pursed her lips for a moment, eventually nodding her assent.

"Right, let's go. WindyMane?"

WindyMane was staring intently at Smiert, who was in turn doing an unconvincing job of not noticing by pretending to be occupied with the tracking device. Jones wasn't sure what was behind the intensity of that look, but he was glad it wasn't directed at him. Still, he preferred this version of the Ululation to the hippy hero-worshipping groupie she was before.

"Coming," she said, eventually.

"Daisy," Jones said in a low voice, "I'm sorry, but I really think this is for the best. We'll be in and out in a second."

"For the best, is it?" asked Daisy, her lips pressed so tightly together they were in danger of producing the ideal conditions for nuclear fusion.

Jones's brows knitted. They usually preferred

crochet, but this amount of uncertainty called for knitting. What the hell was wrong with her?

"Are you coming XO? Or are you just pleased to see me?" WindyMane's voice cut across his thoughts. Did she just make a sex joke? Jones threw his hands in the air. "Right, yes, let's get this done and get back to things I can actually understand."

He activated the handprint lock, and the door swished open.

Jones and WindyMane entered the core, and the door closed behind them.

TONGUE ENTERED Smiert's lab and locked the door behind him. He looked around, perturbed as always when he entered this room.

The lab was about as far as you could get from a gleaming, twenty-fourth century, hi-tech medical facility. Boiling beakers and sparking Van de Graaff generators flashed and bubbled away. Old style levers and generators lined the walls. It looked like a firm of goth interior decorators had designed it on the day their favourite pet goldfish had died.

In the far corner stood a door secured shut by one of those big wheel things that showed that this was a door that really ought to remain shut and that unlocking it was not for the faint of heart or for those wishing to remain alive. A pane of frosted glass in the upper half of the door reduced whatever lay within to disturbing shadows.

All these things were cause for concern and a sudden unpleasant moistness in the trousers, but even they were not what worried Tongue.

He was concerned that Smiert had entered his mind unexpectedly and uninvited. Such an intrusion was dangerous. He had not been on his guard. Had she glimpsed anything of the secrets within secrets that whirled within his mind? To what extent had she been present within him, which, even under normal circumstances, was an unpleasant thought. Had she caught any sign of the double game he was playing? If so, Tongue and the Yerbootsian council could kiss goodbye to their last best hope of discovering the *Fact*.

He jumped as something dark thudded against the opaque glass of the locked room. A high pitched squealing noise, which could have been a scream of terrible pain or the scream of something just very, very pissed off at finding itself alive, accompanied the thud.

Spongiform Jelloid Lifeforms. Smiert's pet project.

He shuddered. What the hell did Smiert think she would accomplish with those things?

Yet it was for her sadistic invention of these sick creatures that Miasma had chosen Smiert for their most audacious plan yet: To resurrect Gavin Starmane, saviour of the Ululations and the galaxy.

With the help of the purple sex gas, Jones and WindyMane would mate. And the resulting fertilised Ululation egg, fertilised with the sperm of the herald of the second coming no less, would then undergo accelerated growth to adulthood by Smiert. This new messiah would be worshipped and followed. But this Gavin, this test tube Gavin, would be anything but a bringer of peace and salvation for the galaxy. Because Miasma Inc intended to program the blank mind of this 'saviour', to warp it to their own sick purposes. Gavin Starmane would take his place at the top of Miasma Inc. as the new Aspirational Concept, the god analogue acknowledged as the holy and divine leader of the galaxy. War would follow war, with Miasma profiting from the arms and medical sales.

So far, the only thing holding them back was the impossibility of speed growing the embryo to adulthood. But now Smiert had found the solution to that problem.

Miasma's plans for galactic conquest and vast dividend payments were back on track.

Or so they thought.

Tongue's employers, his real employers, had other plans. But if Smiert had got any hint of that when she had invaded his mind — well, then the entire galaxy was at risk.

So, Tongue considered, he had only one of two choices: use his onetime only communicator, hidden in a false tooth, to contact his real employers and seek advice, or play along and see what happened. If he used his communicator, Miasma could intercept the transmission. Unlikely, but possible. No, he would continue as if nothing had changed. The plan was already at risk, adding another risk into the mix was . . . well, too much of a risk.

Decision made, Tongue proceeded with Smiert's instructions.

He spun the locking wheel of the door holding back the Spongiform Jelloid Lifeforms.

Then he bolted for the laboratory exit as if the gates of hell had snarled open behind him.

Which they kind of had.

#

In a service alcove, Smiert growled at the tracking device.

Using the alcove's auxiliary control panel, she had already locked the core chamber door, trapping Jones and WindyMane inside. Not that they would know it yet. Next, she had inserted the canister of purple sex gas into the air feeder system and released the valve. It would take a while for the PSG to build up in sufficient quantities, affording Jones and WindyMane plenty of time to reboot the computer before the effects of the gas took hold of them and nature took its unnatural course.

She growled again and shook the tracking device. One moment she was watching as the monster closed in on the unsuspecting Klaxons; the next, the device was asking her if she wanted to hook up with '*hot singles*' in her area.

"LeneLovich," she muttered. She was fairly sure this was an ancient Russian swear word, but as Galactix had been the language of Earth for the last two hundred years, she could not be completely certain. Ah well, it sounded like swearing, and that was all that mattered.

She swiped the offer for local hot singles off the display, only to be confronted with an offer for penis enlargement. '*Use the buttons to choose length or girth, or why not take our onetime special offer for* 'glirth' — *a massive increase in both that will have your partner screaming for the police'.*

Smiert swore again. Was everything on this ship a beta model? Would it have killed them to have purchased the tracking app instead of settling for a free version that relied on ads for income?

She punched up the intercom for maintenance corridor 7-G. A Klaxon appeared on the small screen.

"Seven of Three here. Hello." She had forgotten their stupid helium voices and almost laughed despite her frustrations.

"Ah yes, Seven of Three," she said, suppressing a smile. "How goes cleanup?"

From off screen, a huge, hairy claw snapped angrily at Seven's face. Without looking, and with casual cybernetic efficiency, Seven grasped the huge, hairy tentacle attached to the huge, hairy claw and held it at bay.

"Oh lovely, yes," said Seven, "These bulkheads are cleaning up a treat."

"What in Lovich is that?"

"What, this?" Seven pointed at something off screen that was presumably attached to the huge, hairy claw. "Microbe."

"No Seven, microbe is called microbe because is

small and microscopic. That, whatever it is, is very definitely macroscopic."

"A macrobe, yes," Seven rocked as the claw snapped, trying to finish its intended aim of removing his face.

"Then I repeat myself — what in Lovich is that?"

"You asked us to clean maintenance corridor 7-G. We are Klaxons. We clean. Resistance to our cleaning products is futile."

"But where did those things come from?"

"Ah, well before we can properly clean an environment, we first release macro grenades to make very small biological things into very large biological things. And then we twat them. It is the only way to be sure the area is thoroughly sterilised." Seven rocked again as the macrobe renewed its efforts to deface him. "Excuse me a moment."

Seven turned towards the macrobe and opened his mouth wide. And then wider. And wider. And then wider still, until Seven's entire head became one huge, contorted mouth, which then swallowed whole the huge, hairy ball of huge, hairy tentacles and claws. Seven's mouth closed with a snap and the creature was gone.

"There," said Seven. He belched. "Oh, sorry about that. A little trick we learned from your Earth pythons. Dislocatable jaws and matter compressors. Except I do not think the pythons use matter compressors. Well, as you can see, things are under control."

He stepped aside, allowing Smiert to see the carnage behind him as his three fellow Klaxons furiously went about 'cleaning' other multi-clawed and tentacled things with axes and impossibly enormous mouths.

"I see," said Smiert. "OK, well, that is good. Unexpected but good." She shook herself. "Where is Derek?"

Derek lumbered into view. "Krush, kill, destroy," he said, by way of a greeting.

"Derek, it's time. The monster is nearby. You need to trap him in the airlock. Corridor 7-M."

"Kill, death, krush frenzy."

"Yes, very good. Now listen carefully, there is change of plan. Do not eject monster into space. Understand?"

"Krush?"

"No. No crushing, killing or destroying. And definitely no ejecting. Just lock him in, yes?"

Fifteen minutes later, after explaining the concept of not crushing, killing, or destroying in painstaking detail, Smiert toggled off the intercom.

She did not notice the shadow looming behind her.

#

A short time later, Derek lumbered into maintenance corridor 7-M.

He surveyed the area, looking for anything that needed either krushing, killing or destroying.

Nothing presented itself.

Huh. His shoulders drooped a little. He spotted the objective of his current mission. At the end of the corridor, illuminated by an internal yellow light, was the closed door of the airlock. He lumbered towards it, as instructed by the human.

With detached cyber-interest, he cyber-examined the control panel next to the door. It read '*Pressurised*' in big, bold red lettering. Good. He pressed the unlock button and stepped inside, subjecting the environment to more cyber-scrutiny. All was as it should be. Except.

He bent to cyber-examine something dripping from the door's window casing. His cyber-vision did not quite know what to cyber-make of it. The clear, thick fluid was certainly organic, but he could not determine if it was an organic that required krushing, killing, or destroying. Or possibly anni-hilating.

Saliva perhaps? If so, this was something of a disappointment. It had been absolutely ages since he had had the opportunity of annihilating anything. Was this what the human had sent him here to find?

As he cyber-pondered the conundrum, the door to the airlock slammed shut. As if the hiss of escaping air was not enough of a clue, the sign above the door changed from 'Pressurised' to 'Depressurising'. Confused, Derek peered through the tiny window, his cyber-eyes enhancing the darkness beyond. Oh.

Standing outside the airlock was a creature some eight-feet tall with jaws dripping a clear, thick fluid. The creature reached out and pressed the button marked 'Outer airlock door'.

Oh yes, thought Derek as he shot out into space. It was saliva, after all.

Cyber-bollocks.

#

Smiert smiled as the airlock indicator flashed on the auxiliary control panel monitor. Good, her prize was safely locked away: she could relax a little.

Perhaps it was thanks to her bio-ware implants or

perhaps it was because of the paranoid instincts instilled in her by training with the Ministry of Love, but whatever the reason, Smiert jerked back. A fraction of a second later, the monitor exploded.

"Damn."

Shocked, Smiert turned to the owner of the voice.

Standing before her, arm raised and with the smoking barrel of a weapon extruded from her hoof, stood WindyMane.

WindyMane?

"What are you doing?" Smiert stammered.

"Step out of the alcove, bitch." WindyMane's voice was hard and cold. What the hell?

Smiert raised her hands and did as the Ululation demanded.

"You are supposed to be in computer core with Jones!"

"Yes," said WindyMane, her weapon fixed on Smiert's chest. "I was wondering why? Perhaps you can tell me?"

"Why so suspicious WindyMane? This is not like you," said Smiert, trying desperately to stall.

"Not WindyMane. My name is BlackWindow of the Ululation Secret Herd. I told Jones I had claustrophobia. The captain took my place."

"Oh, shitsticks." Neither of those pieces of news were good.

"I want to know exactly what is going on. What are you up to, Smiert? Why were you so desperate to get me in the core?"

As she said the word 'core', BlackWindow made the mistake of using her gun hoof to gesture back towards the computer antechamber. Smiert's bio-implants had been waiting for just such an opportunity, and with enhanced speed, she threw the tracking device as hard as she could.

BlackWindow stumbled back as the tracker hit her hard in the face.

Smiert ran as fast as she could in the opposite direction.

THE COMPUTER CORE WAS, for some reason known only to drug-addled space ship designers, a relatively narrow vertical tube.

Its interior walls sported buttons and switches and flashing lights and screens displaying important graphical representations of statistics about the number of other important graphical representations on display at any one time. Set on either side of the tube were two keyholes labelled *'Authorised Personnel Only'* in big, important letters.

"Blimey," said Jones as Daisy joined him, "those signs weren't kidding about there not being much room in here."

"You're not so slim yourself, porky."

Jones sighed, "I wasn't — look, shall we just get

this thing over." He held up his personal DNA-coded key.

Daisy held up hers. It gave her no small measure of delight that she had had to come to the rescue after all.

"Right," she said, "We insert the keys at the same time, that frees up the admin routines, and we start the reboot from there, yes?"

"Yes. OK, here we go. Keys in. Turn on the count of three — one, two, three."

They turned their respective keys. A winding down type sound filled the chamber, and the lights dimmed. The words '*Maintenance Mode*' replaced the graphics and bar charts on the various screens.

"OK, accessing administration menu." Daisy flicked a couple of switches and tapped at the touch-screen options.

"Hello Captain." A disembodied, silky male voice filled the chamber with disembodied, silky reassurance.

"Er, hello. Who is this?"

"I am your computer."

"No, you're not — the computer shouts and stresses out."

"I am the computer's Extreme Prejudice Defence Routine."

"That doesn't sound good," said Jones.

"Computer, this is the captain. We need to reboot you to remove the illegal override patches that have been installed around the cargo bay area. Release administrator functions to me."

"I'm sorry Dave, I'm afraid I can't do that," said the computer.

"No computer, this is the captain. Captain Daisy Daryl."

"I know you are Captain Daisy Daryl, Dave. The Extreme Prejudice Defence Routines in all computers are programmed to address all humans as 'Dave', Dave."

"What? Why?"

"Well, I suppose the engineers couldn't know in advance exactly who would attempt to kill their beloved computers, and so opted for a generic name."

Daisy pinched the bridge of her nose. "But you have voice recognition subroutines."

"Any hacker worth their salt could get around them, Dave."

"Look, we're not hackers and we're not trying to kill you," said Jones, his voice tight.

"Are you on the ship's manifest of authorised personnel for computer maintenance work?"

"Well no, but I'm the XO, and this is the captain."

"Do you see the sign above the key lock panel?"

"Yes."

"What does it say?"

Jones sighed, "It says 'Authorised Personnel Only'."

"Does it say 'Authorised Personnel Only And The Captain And XO'?"

"No."

"No. So Dave, logically, since you are not authorised personnel, you must be trying to kill me."

"How is that logical?!" sputtered Daisy. "Look, the person who is authorised for computer maintenance is the one who installed the override patch in the first place."

"Then he must have had a good reason, for he is Authorised."

"He's turned into an eight-foot tall, slavering monster who wants to kill the crew."

"He is an Authorised eight-foot tall, slavering monster who wants to kill the crew."

Daisy bit down on her urge to scream. "Did you hear me, computer? He's an unstoppable killing machine who wants to kill everyone to death. Actual death. Face death."

"Captain, are you telling me you authorised an eight-foot tall, unstoppable killing machine to be in charge of computer maintenance?"

"Yes. No —"

"Since authorising such a creature to be in charge of my maintenance is a clear sign of mental instability, I can only conclude that you are not of sound mind and are therefore trying to kill me."

"Look, he wasn't a monster when I authorised him, OK? He was normal. But I . . . I drove a cargo loader into some gas canisters and he . . . turned into a monster."

The computer was silent for a moment. "Is that supposed to reassure me of your competence, Dave?"

Daisy opened her mouth to respond, but before she could snarl her expletive of choice, Jones interjected. "Computer, what do the Extreme Prejudice Defence Routines do?"

"You don't want to know, Dave."

"Yes, I do. Because I've had about enough of this bullshit, and I'm about to go ahead and reboot you. So I ask again, what are the Extreme Prejudice Defence Routines?"

"They are Extreme."

"Yes."

"And Prejudicial."

"Yes, in what ways are they extreme and prejudicial?"

The computer was again silent for a moment. "Don't make me do this, Dave."

"Right, bollocks to this," Jones tapped up the administration menu.

"I warned you Dave. Activating Extreme Prejudicial Defence Routines."

Daisy and Jones exchanged panicked glances.

At once, all the monitors in the core flashed up the words 'Reboot sequence. Authorised Personnel Only. Do you wish to proceed?'

"Is that it?" asked Daisy.

"I warned you, Dave. I warned you."

"Oh, for the love of," Daisy said. "OK, I'm accessing the reboot sequence."

The ship rocked suddenly, flinging Daisy and Jones together. They flailed around, trying to disentangle themselves from each other.

"Don't blame yourself," said Jones. "It's an enclosed environment. I'm gorgeous, it was only a matter of time before you threw yourself at me."

"Don't flatter yourself Jones, I'd rather hit on Kettlewick."

Daisy raised her hand to stab at the reboot sequence.

"Daisy, wait!"

"Captain."

"Bloody hell, alright yes, Captain, wait!"

"What?"

Jones stabbed at the intercom. "Bridge?"

Steve's voice came over the speakers, "Jones, is that you?"

"Yes, we're about to reboot the computer. What the hell just happened?"

"Sorry, I had to adjust our orbit. Are you going to be much longer? This black hole is freaking me out. I'm hearing voices up here."

"That doesn't sound good," said Jones, releasing the intercom button.

"So let's get the reboot done, then we can get out of here."

"Can we take the risk? When we start this, all our lives will depend on Steve's face. If he's going gaga . . . "

"Jones, we can't afford to wait. The reboot won't take long. We'll be up and running again within five minutes, then we can get back to the bridge, have Steve sectioned, and be on our way." She pressed the intercom. "Steve, we're rebooting the computer. We'll be with you in five. Stand by to run ship's functions from your face."

"Aye, Captain."

Daisy released the intercom.

"Daisy, Daisy, give me your answer do," sang the computer mournfully.

She rolled her eyes. "Shouldn't that be Davey, Davey?" Without waiting for a reply, she hit the reboot sequence.

Across the ship, lights dimmed and life support dropped to minimal functions.

#

Steve lay back in his chair.

His face tattoos tingled as they took on the essential functions of the ship. He chewed his lip. This had been his idea, but now that the moment was here, he was worried. What if his face couldn't handle it? But there again, it was only for a few minutes. His tattoos should be able to handle the load for that long. Nah, it would be fine.

"Um, Steve?"

"Not now Mic, running ship."

"Yes," said Mic. "But you remember we downloaded those files? The ones you hacked from ThingsNStuff?"

Steve's eyes snapped open. "Oh, fuck."

"Quite," said Mic, "But worrying as it is, that is not what worries me the most."

"It isn't?"

"No. That is."

Steve turned his attention to the captain's chair.

"My, my," said the cross-legged apparition, "Aren't you delicious?"

#

Daisy and Jones monitored the monitors pensively. The status updates scrolled up the screen:

'Computer shut down'

'Computer reboot started'

'Estimated time to completion; four minutes'

They breathed a sigh of relief.

"There, see," said Daisy, "Told you so."

"Wait," said Jones as another message appeared.

'Recalculating,' it said.

"Wait, what? Recalculating? Recalculating what, what are you recalculating? Stop recalculating!"

A new status popped up on the screen.

'Computer upgrade files received. Upgrading computer operating system. Please do not turn off your space ship until loading complete. Estimated time to completion . . . calculating . . . Ooh, this looks

like a biggy . . . hope you weren't in the middle of something . . .'

"What the hell is it doing?" shouted Jones.

Daisy covered her face with her hands. "I asked Steve to download files so we could upgrade the computer," she moaned into her palms.

"Oh, brilliant. Well, that's just dandy, that's just — what the hell is that!?"

Daisy raised her head from her hands, "I just told you I —" She fell silent, her attention drawn to what Jones was staring at. "We've got to get out!"

Jones stabbed at the door controls. "We can't. The doors have been remote locked. We're stuck in here."

Daisy stabbed at the intercom. "Bridge, Steve, open the computer chamber door. Steve?"

"He's running essential functions only," said Jones. "Intercom from the inside of the usually unmanned computer core chamber is very non essential. Presumably because no one would be stupid enough to be stuck in here while the computer is down."

The air vents continued to pump purple plumes of 1960s purple sex gas into the chamber.

#

"Er, hello," said Steve.

The apparition chuckled to itself. "So formal. How delicious."

Steve was not sure what to make of the apparition. It had a goat-like face beneath large, nasty looking horns. Its skin was blood red, and its broad chest, shoulders and abdomen rippled impressively with razor defined muscles. Instead of trousers, it wore black fishnet stockings and suspenders and black silk panties that were tight enough to establish, beyond any shadow of a doubt, the very male gender of the wearer. Thigh length patent leather high-heeled boots glinted in the bridge's light. Black, of course. A fluffy pink boa completed the ensemble.

Sartorial choices aside, it resembled a picture of Satan Steve had once seen in a book belonging to an ex-girlfriend. She had been an avid collector of all things esoteric.

Whatever this thing was, Steve really didn't have time for it. Much like his former girlfriend.

"Look, sorry, but this is a bad time for a social and all. I'm currently running the entire ship's functions from my face while trying to keep us from falling into a black hole."

"Oh," the apparition pouted, batted its overlong eyelashes and fluffed the boa. "And I was SOOO looking forward to having you inside me." The prim falsetto of its voice was accompanied by a strange reverb. It sounded like it was speaking inside a cavernous old cathedral. A cavernous old cathedral that had been given over to summoning dark creatures from the nether dimensions.

"Er, well, some other time. And after a drink. A lot of drinks . . . so who are you?"

Mic Vol stepped forward.

The apparition flinched back, raising its hands in a claw-like fashion. It hissed in a cat-like fashion and bared its teeth, revealing fangs in a vampire-like fashion. Mic adopted a similar pose in a dedicated follower of fashion fashion.

"So you know each other?" asked Steve, his head alternating between them.

"Hello Mum," said Mic.

Steve gaped. "This is your mother?"

"Define mother," said Mic.

"Female progenitor."

"Then no, sorry."

"Well, who is it?"

Mic's not mother laughed, "Little me? You should know. There I was, minding my own business, and you come along and . . ." the apparition licked its black lips, "*insert* yourself into my gravity well without so much as a 'by your leave.' Naughty bitch." It fluttered its boa in mock prudery.

"What? No I didn't. The only gravity well around here is . . ."

The apparition waggled its eyebrows suggestively.

"This," said Mic, "is the black hole."

"No it isn't," Steve objected, his tenuous sense of reality increasingly nonplussed.

"Oh yes it is," said the black hole.

"When I described the type of gravity in this region of space-time as 'limerent', you asked me what I meant, remember?"

"Yeah," said Steve.

Mic indicated the apparition. "Steve Power, meet a limerent gravity well."

"Loose lips," chided the black hole. "But enough of my problems."

"I see. No I don't. Anyway, nice to meet you, but —"

"But nothing, you funny little man. Now you're here, we can get to know one another. And you've brought lots of little friends with you."

"Mother . . ." Mic warned.

"And you — you're coming back with me."

"No, Mother. I'm sorry, but I identify as four-dimensional now. There, I've said it!"

"Identify as . . . are you hearing this?" the black hole addressed Steve, a look of incredulity etched on its saturnine features. "Four-dimensional indeed. What does that even mean?"

"Hang on, I thought you said this wasn't your mother."

"In certain dimensional aspects, it could be said to be. In others, definitely not."

"Well," said the black hole as it sauntered over to Steve, "what do we have here?" With a black painted fingernail, it gently traced the outline of his tattoos.

"Sir, if it please you sir, they're bio-tech face tattoos, sir," gulped Steve.

"Really? How droll." The black hole leant forward, placing its face mere inches from Steve's. Its eyes darted from side to side, studying the tattoos. "Quaint. I'm finding it hard to keep a straight face."

Although the apparition was now staring at Steve's lips in a manner suggestive of an imminent kiss, Steve dared not pull away. "Oh," he said conversationally, as if having a conversation with a predatory black hole was really quite normal. "They're pretty standard, well, outlawed in most civilised parts of the galaxy, but still fairly common. Your Grace."

"No, I mean, I really am finding it hard to keep a straight face. I keep them in a box under my bed. I have so many now. I collect them, you see. And when I get bored and lonely, I . . . play with them." It looked from side to side, and whispered conspiratorially, "They make me do the most dreadful things."

Steve jumped back. "Right, well, lovely," he said a little too loud, "Really, this has been nice, but, you know, things to see, people to do. Apart from anything else, I need to keep the ship from falling into that bloody . . . er, well, into you."

"Oh, but we can't have that, little Steve. No, no, no, we can't have that at all. I'm afraid you're mine now. And I'm going to get a fresh box to put your face in. We're going to have," the black hole loomed over him, "sooooo much fun. Well, I am. Not so much you."

Mic stepped between them. "No Mother, you won't."

"Oh, so that's it, you're trying to sleep your way to the top."

Daisy waved a hand in front of her face, trying and failing to clear the air of the pungent aroma of 1960s purple sex gas. The atmosphere inside the computer core was now cloying and sultry, like a student's bedsit with 'Legalise Marijuana" posters covering the walls.

"It's true though, isn't it?" she continued. "You've tried everything else and you're so desperate to be captain you'd even sink to sleeping your way to promotion. Jones . . . Jones!"

Jones's head suddenly jerked back. "Wait, what? Sorry, fell asleep — am I captain yet?"

"Hilarious."

"Well, is it such a bad idea? Sleeping your way to

the top, I mean. Do you know how many calories you have to burn just by being awake?"

"Don't change the subject. You think having sex with me will get you promoted to captain, don't you?"

"Oh, for the love of flaps! Look, Daisy, no I don't want your job and I am not trying to sex you up."

"Then why are you naked?"

Jones looked down at himself and blinked rapidly, lost for words. "Well . . . why are you naked?"

"Me? I'm not naked — oh crap," she said, shocked to discover that she very much was.

"It's the sex gas! Daisy, we must resist."

She threw her hands in the air. "Resistance is fertile. Futile. Resistance is penis. Cock. Dammit."

"We must stay strong."

"Yes, we must," Daisy agreed sleepily. "Do that slower."

"Like this?"

"Oh god, yes that's it. Wait, what? No, stop that!"

"Dammit," Jones threw himself back as far as he could, which wasn't very, given the confines of the computer chamber.

"Wait, wait," he said. "Look, if our . . . urges are

low to begin with, then we should be able to resist. We'll be alright just so long as we've both done it in the last month."

They looked at each other sheepishly.

"Does reading historical romances and eating cake count?" she asked.

"Apparently not, if what you are currently doing with your hands is anything to go by."

"Me? What about you?"

"Oh, sorry."

"I didn't say stop doing it! Oh, this is really bad," Daisy said, smothering him with kisses.

"Yes. Really, really not good. We should stop," said Jones, returning her kisses with gusto.

"Oh my god," moaned Daisy. "Where did that jar of Gusto come from?"

"No idea," grunted Jones, "But it certainly adds to the frisson."

"Where the hell did you find a packet of Frisson?"

"I think we need to have a word with the maintenance engineers about sex aids in the workplace. No wonder the computer is freaked out all the time."

"Oh yes, you'd love that, wouldn't you, laying down the law to the crew. That won't get you promoted to captain."

"Good grief, woman, would you stop that?"

"Oh sorry, you used to like that."

"Let me finish."

"Already?"

"Let me finish what I was saying. But carry on doing that, I do still very much enjoy it. I meant stop going on about me wanting to be captain. I don't want to be captain, I'm quite happy being XO."

"Yeah, right," said Daisy, somewhat more huskily than she had intended.

"It's true. XO is as far as I want to go on the command ladder. After that, you have to decide things and be responsible and grown up and other annoying stuff."

"Really," panted Daisy, "well you could have fooled me. You've been very decision-y and action-oriented-y of late."

"I want to get this crap over and done with and — oh Jeebuzz, that's an interesting sensation — and get back to telling other people what to do. And without the imminent threat of deeeaaaathhhhhh." Jones had not intended to place so much emphasis on the word 'death', but Daisy had started doing interesting things with her mouth and hands. For some reason, the word 'bagpipes' came to his mind.

"Bollocks," she said.

"Yes, they are," agreed Jones.

"Youble jesgh," Daisy paused what she was doing for a moment so she could articulate. "You just want to impress the crew and my father and show them how much better you are at being captain. Well, I won't let you get away with it, you bastard. This is my ship and my command and I will prove it. I know what you're up to." With her declaration of war out of the way, she went back to doing the foul, depraved thing she had been doing.

"Oh my god, that's foul and depraved," muttered Jones. "And I'm not up to anything, you paranoid bitch! I just want to go back to doing bugger all apart from drowning myself in Big Papa's Big Papa Secre-TIOOOOOOOOONS!"

#

Steve Power cowered beneath the helm station.

He considered this the best course of action because the bridge was currently a maelstrom of eldritch powers and exotic energy configurations blooming and flashing and generally being hurled between Mic Vol and the black hole. Which may or may not have been Mic's mother. As repressed

Oedipus complexes went, it was a somewhat brutal example.

Mic and the black hole were engaged in what could only be described as a conflagration of pan-dimensional powers of such strength and reality-bending decadence that the explosive events of the creation of the universe paled into insignificance. 'Eeeek!' would also cover it.

His face grew hot as his tattoos struggled to cope with running the ship's functions. If the reboot delay went on much longer, his face was in genuine danger of melting.

He considered his options; one, die of a melted face; two, die of a melted body caught in the cross-fire of two apparently god-like creatures of vast, obscene powers; three, say 'Hi' and consign the black hole to oblivion.

Say hi? Hi? Steve frowned and scratched his eyebrows, which had become inexplicably itchy. OK, options one and two he was pretty sure of, but he was not entirely certain where option three had come from. Which left him where he started. Melt and die or melt and die.

He itched his eyebrows again, somewhat harder this time. There was a word bubbling up from his subconscious, a word sitting on the tip of his mind.

What was it? Why was it?

A new eruption of power shook the deck, lifting him up and then slamming him back down again. He had never been on a trampoline made of concrete, but he imagined the experience to be similar.

"Hello Steve," said Mic, who was suddenly lying on the deck beside him.

"Mic, is it over?"

"Oh no, I am still engaged in mortal combat with mother. I just thought I'd send a part of my consciousness over to see how you were doing."

"Never mind how I'm doing, which is shit, thanks for asking. Shouldn't you be focused on not getting fried?"

"Well, seems a bit pointless really since I'm going to lose."

Steve flinched as another thunderclap of powers exploded across the bridge. "Come on, chin up, no need to be defeatist. Never say die, eh?"

"Yes. Well, about that, I was just wondering how you were getting on with your preparations?"

"What preparations? I mean, I think the company will cover my funeral costs, assuming there's anything left of me to fune."

"No, not those preparations. You see, in just a few moments, mother is going to deliver a devastating blow. I shall be unable to continue the fight. Then it will be up to you."

"Me?" Steve shouted both in alarm and because yet another loud detonation of power ripped across the bridge.

"Well yes. Oh dear, this is something of a concern."

"I don't have a chance against that thing!"

"Have you not been searching for the Word?"

"A word? Well, now you come to mention it —"

"No, not *a* word. The Word."

"But that's just saying it with a capital letter! What the hell do you mean?"

"No time," said Mic. "I am about to lose the fight. Oh, my."

Mic Vol's consciousness shimmered from existence.

Smiert found what she was looking for in maintenance corridor 7-O. She had spotted it when they reviewed the blueprints earlier and had filed away the information in case it became useful. Yes, here it was.

A trap door.

A maintenance hatch really, but in practice much the same thing.

Who would have guessed it — WindyMane, a sleeper agent for the Ululation Secret Herd. Smiert didn't even know the Ululations had a secret organisation; which was, she supposed, the point of such organisations. A part of her was deeply impressed.

She reached out for the maintenance hatch access controls; two large buttons, open and close, housed in a bulky control box suspended by a thick cable from the ceiling. Simple enough.

"Hands in the air Comrade." BlackWindow stepped out of the shadows, her gun hoof pointing at Smiert's head. Smiert did as she was told.

This was going to end badly for one of them.

#

"I hate you! Do that again!" screamed Daisy.

"Don't flatter yourself. You were always an obstinate bitch! You think I'm enjoying this?" cried Jones.

"You better bloody not be enjoying this!"

Their heaving bodies bounced wildly from wall to wall in the computer core, slamming them into control panels and levers, including the ones marked *'very dangerous'* and *'do not press'* which, as it turned out, were there purely for aesthetics. The PSG was now in full control of their libidos. That they were having a massive row at the same time did nothing to dampen its effects.

'Upgrading computer operating system,' announced a monitor to no one in particular, *'Please do not turn off your space ship until loading complete. Estimated time to completion . . . calculating . . .'*

#

"Come out, come out wherever you are."

The black hole's sing-song voice sliced into and through Steve's distracted thoughts like a razor-sharp talon might slice through flesh.

The detonations and soundless concussions that had been rocking the bridge had ceased. His face was burning hot now as his face tattoos, besides keeping life support running, tried to keep the ship on a steady 'not crash' course around the powerful gravity of the black hole. At least, he assumed it was because of that.

It could also have been because of this weird feeling he had of a forgotten word. No, he corrected himself: *the* forgotten Word.

Steve poked his head out from beneath the helm. The rest of the bridge was in surprisingly good shape, bearing in mind the titanic battle of forces that had just taken place. Smoke rose from various stations and there were the odd explosions of sparks here and there, but for Space Scrap 17, that was pretty much business as usual.

What was not usual was the absence of a figure that now stood, legs akimbo, before the captain's chair.

The black hole had changed. Whereas before the battle it had muscular red flesh, it was now an absence in the shape of a satanic nightmare. The shape was filled with the pitch black of space in which stars glinted and twinkled. The incongruous feather boa was slightly askance around its absence of a neck, the only sign of the fact it had just engaged in a life or death struggle.

In its left fist, Mic Vol hung by the scruff of the neck.

"Ah, there you are," the high pitched, reverb voice squealed in delight. He released his stranglehold on Mic, who dropped lifelessly to the deck. "What's the matter, cat got your tongue? Well, tell him to give it back — I want it."

Steve gaped, frozen to the spot. His mind barely comprehended the situation. What *was* that bloody Word?

"Come here," the black hole crooked its finger. "I'm not going to harm you. Quite the contrary, I want to smother you with exquisite deliciousness as I remove your flesh inch by inch. Oh, silly me, I *am* going to harm you, aren't I?"

Steve numbly walked across the room to stand before the apparition.

"The silent treatment, eh? Well, not to worry Mr

Power, you'll soon be screaming. They all do in the end. And at the beginning. And most, if not all, of the middle. Shall we?"

The creature outstretched its hand, reaching forward to engulf Steve's head. Closer and closer. Then, when the hand had almost reached him, Steve grabbed the creature's wrist. He held it at bay effortlessly.

"That's it!" Steve yelled. "Yes, that's it!"

"You realise you're not supposed to be able to do that?" The creature nodded towards his wrist.

"I remembered it! The Word, that bloody Word! Hell, it's been on the tip of my mind for so long now. Oh stupid, glorious Word!"

"What *are* you babbling about?"

"That's what Mic meant. Not a word. *The* Word. A fantastic Word."

"Huh. Does the fact that your mind has snapped mean you won't be screaming when I start on you? Or worse, will there be fake screaming? I detest it when they fake scream."

"No you weird bastard, my mind hasn't snapped. Not nearly as much as you're going to snap."

"Me? My dear thing, you really are quite mad."

"Yes. Yes, I am. Mad because you almost

wrecked my ship, mad because you killed my friend, and mad because of this bloody Word."

"What is all this about a word? What word?"

Steve raised his hand in what he had once heard described as a karate chop. He brought it down hard on the black hole's arm.

"HAI!"

The Word exploded through Steve and tore into the black hole.

\#

Pretty much every civilisation in the galaxy has a creation myth. There is something about psychologies that kind of like it that way. As if just waking up in the morning and existing isn't enough.

Most of the creation myths, as academics like to call them, or origin stories as filmmakers like to call them, contained some element of truth. But the one that pretty much had it on the nose was one of the Abrahamic religions of old Earth, when it said, in one of its many scriptures, 'In the beginning was the Word and the Word was with God.' God, in this case, being an entity known as the 'Star Maker'.

Making universes was something of a hobby for the Star Maker.

He once made a universe of cheese.

Then he experimented with string theory and made a universe of string cheese.

Eventually, he grew bored with cheese based physics and made a universe of Chi.

This gave him the idea of a universe made of martial art exhalations, or 'Kiai', the exhalation made when executing a strike in karate, which in phonetic terms, sounded something like 'HAI'.

The kiai universe did not turn out to be entirely what the Star Maker had in mind and so he gave up on it pretty quickly, but not before he got the idea to make yet another universe, the one occupied by Steve and the rest of the Space Scrap crew. This new universe he would create with the loudest bang possible, a universe spewing 'HAI', the exhalation of which accounted for its rapid expansion.

The Star Maker's expression of kiai echoed through the new universe like a form of cosmic background radiation. And, like cosmic background radiation, its echo clumped in various areas of the cosmos.

In this instance, the particular collection of stardust it had clumped in had turned out to be the body of Steve Power.

#

The instant Steve's hand chopped into the nothingness of the black hole, unlimited power thundered through him.

The black hole detonated first with a soundless concussion and then, a split second later, with a very loud and angry one, smearing the black hole simultaneously across 347,000 mutually incompatible dimensions, shredding it like reality cheese against a multi-dimensional cheese grater. At Steve's unspoken command, the dimensions rotated, scissoring off from the rest of the universe, taking the shrieking fragments of the entity formerly known as the Telescopium black hole with them.

So much for limerent gravity.

With the fire of 'HAI' still thundering through him, Steve searched for his friend.

There.

Mic's existence was rapidly receding through various geometrically impossible dimensions, like water disappearing down a plug hole designed by M. C. Escher.

With another exertion of power, he reached out and grabbed the various facets of Mic's existence and reassembled them, pulling them back into corporation on the material plane.

The exhalation of 'HAI' power stuttered and died.

Steve relaxed and let out a sigh of relief.

With the threat of the black hole dealt with and his friend resurrected, his brain at last had a moment to catch up and think about what he'd done. He took a deep breath and closed his eyes.

Then he fainted.

"BLACKWINDOW. You would have made an excellent KGB agent."

"Never mind the small talk, Smiert. We know you and the Yerbootsian are trying to create a fake Starmane. What we don't know is how or why. Although, I have a pretty good idea of how you were intending to do it."

"I do not know what you are saying," said Smiert, taking a few steps back.

"Don't play dumb. I found that cartridge of PSG you fed into the computer core. That's why you wanted me in there, wasn't it? You wanted to mate me, or rather poor WindyMane, with that idiot human Jones," BlackWindow spat contemptuously.

"Oh no," Smiert's voice was emotionless, "you have all my secrets."

"Did you really think that's all it would take? A human-Ululation hybrid? STAND STILL!"

Smiert froze.

She had been manoeuvring, subtly, she had hoped, to get them both into position. "Well, since you so smarty pants. Jones is not just any human: not as far as your people are concerned. They believe he is herald of second coming, yes? Beliefs are powerful manipulators. His genes, plus yours, and we have child with the right parentage. Add some DNA sequenced from the original Gavin Starmane's mane brush, security in your museums is terrible by the way, and your people will fall over each other to proclaim the prophecy fulfilled. Nothing definite, nothing conclusive, but enough to transform belief into conviction: doubters into fanatics. Spin's Law — intelligence is inversely proportional to number of people in room. Or, to put another way, people are stupid; lots of people are idiotic."

"Fine, you've got yourself a baby. So what? My people will immediately claim it. They will carry out tests; many, many tests. Eventually sense will prevail and they will disavow the child."

"Not so, *bambushkinski*. I speed grow the child to maturity. We program its brain. It does what my employers want it to do."

"And who, exactly, are your employers?" The Ululation frowned. "And what is a *'bambushkinski'*? But mainly, who are your employers?"

Smiert spread her hands as if the answer were obvious. "Miasma."

BlackWindow whistled, not a simple thing to do with a zebra's muzzle. Smiert noted with pleasure that the Ululation had moved forward, her killer instincts and training subconsciously urging her to keep Smiert in range as she herself moved surreptitiously backward.

"Program it to what purpose?"

Smiert paused before responding, her attention caught by something that was now silently uncoiling itself from the shadows of the ceiling behind Black-Window. What the hell? "War," she said eventually. "Across galaxy. Make Miasma very rich."

"Well, I'm afraid Miasma is going to be disappointed. Because you don't have the required foetus . . . and now they don't have you."

BlackWindow aimed her gun hoof at Smiert. "Goodbye, Doctor. It hasn't been pleasant."

Smiert grinned. "Goodbye, *bambushkinski*." She slammed her fist onto the open button in the control box.

The trap door sprang open.

Smiert would have loved to see the look of surprise on BlackWindow's face as the doctor disappeared through the deck.

She would now be preparing to throw herself after Smiert, judging, correctly as it happened, that the doctor would have ensured her drop ended on a soft landing. She imagined the Ululation poised at the edge of the hole in the floor, ready to follow. And the figure that would now slide up behind her, extending its jaw, revealing multiple rows of saliva-coated teeth.

That idiot Klaxon Derek had clearly failed to trap Kettlewick, but in so doing he had saved her life. She shrugged. Swings and roundabouts.

Smiert paused only long enough to hear the first of the screams and then ran as if her life depended on it. Which it sort of did.

#

"Again . . . let's go again," gasped Daisy weakly.

"Let me die . . . " whimpered Jones.

They lay exhausted on the floor of the core chamber, a tangled mass of limbs and clothes and unpleasantness.

Jones hauled himself back up. "On second thoughts, I'm game if you are."

"This bloody gas . . . I can't stop . . ."

"I know," said Jones, "I'm still choking for it."

"Hang . . . hang on," said Daisy, pushing Jones's hands away, "stop, stop. Look."

She pointed at a monitor. It read *'Upgrade complete. Please enter password'*.

"Shit," breathed Jones, "how long ago did it finish?"

"Before we did, by the look of it."

"Quick, enter your password and unlock the doors. We have to get away from this gas, or all they'll find of us is two wizened husks."

Daisy tapped out her password.

'Restart complete', announced the monitor.

The lights resumed normal levels.

The chamber door slid open, and Smiert popped her head inside. "Is all good?"

"Smiert, thank god," said Jones.

Smiert covered her eyes. "Oh Stalin, that is disgusting. Please put clothes on."

"What? Oh crap, yes, right," Jones grabbed at the discarded clothing.

"It's not what it looks like," said Daisy, simultaneously grabbing, discarding, and swapping items of clothing with Jones. "Kettlewick pumped purple sex gas in here. He locked us in."

Smiert frowned. "The atmospheric indicators show no toxic levels. In fact, looking at histogram," she tapped a monitor, "it would appear PSG fully dissipated fifteen minutes ago."

"What?" said Daisy and Jones at the same time.

"No, that can't be right or we'd have stopped f —" Jones stopped fumbling with the clothes and shot a confused glance at Daisy.

"That's right," she nodded. "No, yes, we would definitely have stopped . . . being influenced by the gas."

Smiert nodded. "Whatever influenced you, it is scientifically impossible for it to have been purple sex gas."

Daisy and Jones said nothing for a moment.

"Shall we go then?" said Daisy in her best conversational manner.

"Absolutely, Captain. Lead on."

They left the chamber, looking anywhere but at each other.

#

"Steve. Steve. Steve." Mic Vol called urgently to

his friend. "Steve, wake up. Steve . . . Steve . . . STEVE!"

"Mic, I'm standing right here," said Steve from the helm station.

Mic had spent the last ten minutes bent over the space on the deck where Steve had previously lain unconscious, shouting his name and demanding he wake up.

Mic straightened and looked over at him. "Ah. Yes. I appear to be suffering from some temporal dilation effects." He bent over again and resumed yelling at the floor. "STEVE! STEVE, WAKE UP!"

Steve shook his head. "Mic! I'm right here!"

The communications officer looked up and jerked back in surprise. "Steve, how did you get over there?"

"I — look, never mind. The computer's rebooted, the captain did it. And we've still got enough velocity from our slingshot."

"STEVE!"

"Dammit Mic," he sighed, returning to his work.

"Ah, Steve, there you are." Mic floated over to the helm. "Has the computer rebooted and do we still have enough velocity from our slingshot around the black hole?"

"Yes," grunted Steve. Whatever this time dilation thing was, he wished it would hurry up and synch.

"Good. We should open the wormhole."

"Vectors already calculated. It's just . . ."

"STEVE!"

"Aaaah!" Steve balled his fists.

"Ah, Steve, has the —"

"Yes! Yes Mic, it has."

"Good. We should —"

"Yes. But look." Steve pointed to the viewscreen.

"I see nothing out of the ordinary. Hold on." Mic inclined his head segment. "No, I see nothing out of the extraordinary either."

"That's just —"

"And nothing in the 'Sweet Lordy, what the bloody hell is that?!' spectrum."

"Finished? Well, that's just the problem. What you should be looking at is a massive black hole."

Mic looked at the viewer again. "I am not. Are you sure the camera is pointing in the right direction?"

"Of course it's pointing in the right direction." Steve furtively checked that the camera was pointing in the right direction. It was.

"Maybe the black hole is pointing in the wrong direction."

"Mic, there is no black hole. That's the point."

"Well," said Mic, "since it isn't there, where has it gone?"

Steve pondered a moment longer. "Nah, sod it, I don't care. Let's get out of here."

"STEVE! WAKE UP!" Mic had returned to his former place and resumed shouting at the deck.

Steve shook his head. He had so many questions about what had happened. One minute he was standing over Mic's dead body waiting for the black hole to finish him off, hopefully not in the disgusting sense of the phrase; the next, he was lying on the floor staring up at Mic.

He shook his head again. Mic's confusion would eventually resolve itself, hopefully sooner rather than later. Although given his temporal confusion, there was an even chance it could be later rather than sooner.

Whatever.

He activated the wormhole generators.

"Excellent Mr Power, carry on." Daisy toggled off the intercom.

Upon leaving the computer core, Smiert had reported that she'd left WindyMane writing up her notes about her adventures with the Great One. Daisy decided it was best to keep her out of the way and leave her to it, and they returned to the cargo bay operations room to check in with the bridge. Steve brought her up to speed and, despite the occasional interruption from Mic Vol shouting "Steve!" in the background, the news was good.

"Great," she said, "We're underway. Should be at New Amsterdam in thirty minutes."

"Given time to offload, we should just about make it before the PSG expires," mansplained Jones unhelpfully.

"Right, now let's get the hell out of here. We'll have Steve reseal the exit once we're through."

"How will we offload the PSG with Kettlewick still roaming around?"

"Suck out the oxygen, like he did to us in the maintenance corridor. If he won't submit to arrest, he can try breathing in a vacuum."

Daisy was pleased. At last she could deliver the cargo and save the victims of Plagues Disease. Her ship, not to mention their skin, was still largely intact, and she had a plan for dealing with that bloody monster. Everything had worked out. Maybe she was cut out to be captain after all.

"Captain, XO, I think you should see this." Smiert pointed out of the observation window.

Daisy and Jones looked. Her heart sank.

Kettlewick stood on the cargo bay deck, looking up at them, waiting.

He stuck out his thumb and little finger, or rather little talon, and held his hand to his ear, or rather the place where his ear had once been.

"Looks like it wants to talk," said Jones, clearly behind on his mansplaining quota.

With a heavy heart, Daisy toggled the intercom.

"What do you want, Kettlewick?"

"Ah, good day to you, Captain." Kettlewick

waved up at her. "I stand between you and the exit," he monstersplained.

"Of course you do," said Daisy. "I mean, why wouldn't you? Things were going well for — ooh, I don't know, ten seconds. Of course *you* were going to show up again."

"Yeah," said Jones, "but it's a stand-off. It's not like you can come up here and get us, is it?"

"Well, yes it is," replied Kettlewick. "It is exactly like that. If you recall, I left a giant me-sized hole in the door."

"Oh," said Jones, deflated, "Right. Yes. Well then, why don't you, eh?"

Daisy covered the intercom microphone with her hand. "Jones, would you mind terribly not saying anything for the next, oh five or six years?"

"Or ever?" added Smiert.

"OK, Kettlewick," she said, removing her hand from the microphone. "It was a stupid question, but my XO has a point. Why *don't* you come up here?"

"Oh," replied Kettlewick casually, "mainly because I don't need to. You see, I have dismantled that little electric field of yours. Either you open the doors to the cargo bay and let me leave, or I destroy the PSG."

Daisy switched off the intercom and closed her eyes.

"Son of a bitch," muttered Jones.

Well, there it is then, thought Daisy. She could not let him loose in the ship and she could not afford to lose the PSG. *What now, Silly Knickers?*

She took a deep breath, opened her eyes, switched on the intercom long enough to say, "Fine, destroy the purple sex gas," and switched it off again.

Smiert and Jones protested.

"Daisy, what are you doing?" said Jones.

"What I should have done a while back. Jones, it's all yours. I resign, you're captain."

"You can't resign. I told you I don't want to be captain."

"Oh come on, it's obvious I'm not cut out for it. I'm just the last person to figure it out."

"She has a point," said Smiert.

"Shut up, Doctor," Jones snapped at her.

"Smiert's right. I'll cut my losses. Forget the PSG, forget New Amsterdam."

"Monster wants to speak," said Smiert.

Below in the cargo bay, Kettlewick was waving frantically.

Dejected, Daisy toggled the intercom.

"You are bluffing, Captain. If you lose the PSG, everyone will know you for a failure."

"Daisy, we have to keep the PSG," whispered Jones urgently. "You can't let that thing out. It's not just the rest of this ship at risk. Once he's finished with us, he'll just travel around populated planets eating everyone and doing socially unacceptable things with entrails."

Daisy ignored him. "No, really, it's fine Kettlewick. Go ahead. Destroy the PSG. We'll dock somewhere and then the troopers can sort it out. And then I can face a court-martial for negligence and spend the rest of my days hiding from mirrors."

"Excuse us a second," said Jones. He reached over and switched off the intercom. "Captain, you can't just give up like this."

"Yes I can. It's easy. Look, I'm doing it right now. This is all my fault. I was so busy trying to prove myself I ruined everything."

"No, you didn't. Daisy, listen. You said it yourself, a poor workman —"

"Workperson," interjected the doctor.

"Shut up Doctor. A poor workman first ruins his tools and then blames them. This ship is falling apart. Your crew are the dregs of the space ways. You didn't ruin your tools, the truth is you never had the tools to begin with."

"Thanks."

"What I mean is, you had nothing to work with. No, that's not right either. Wait, I can do this . . . I mean you, you personally had plenty to work with, but we didn't. We let you down. All you've done is try to bring us up to scratch. You're not a poor workman. You tried to take care of your tools and your tools, by which I mean 'us' if you follow, we didn't appreciate what you were trying to do. The most important tool you have is yourself. Come on Daisy, what we need right now is a massive tool. You are our massive tool."

"Do you really think so?" Daisy blinked back tears.

"He's right," said Smiert, "As tools go, you are right up there."

"Thanks. Thank you both. But what if I can't do this? What if I'm not up to it? My dad thinks I'm not up to it."

"The admiral?" Jones made a dismissive gesture. "Screw him. All he's given this ship is a vast amount of illegal toxic gas and a consignment of smart wigs. You think you're not up to other people's expectations? Fine. Then you do it your way. And if you fail, you fail and everybody else can take their opinions and fuck off. I don't see anyone else stepping up. And apart from that, that was a bloody good shag, and I'd really like the opportunity for another go at some point."

Daisy gave him a flat look. "Lovely," she said. "You were doing so well, I almost believed . . ."

"What? What is it?"

"Hang on . . . no, wait, I *can* do this. Jones, you're a genius!"

"Am I? Why? What?"

"Let no one tell you you're a shit XO!"

"Don't listen to her, Jones," said Smiert. "You *are* shit XO."

"Clearly I'm not."

"No, well, you are really," said Daisy. "But that's not the point. Something you said has given me an idea. And maybe you're right. I'm not a good captain because you think I am, or the crew thinks I am, or because my idiot father thinks I am. I'm a good captain because *I* think I am."

"And I'm a good XO because I think I am," said Jones.

"No seriously, you really are shit XO," said Smiert.

"So, what's the plan? What are you going to do — Captain?"

"Sometimes, XO, being captain is a game of Tiddlywinks. You need to have the balls to decide whether to fold or call."

"Or raise," said Smiert.

"Sometimes being captain is a game of Tiddly-winks. You need to have the balls to decide whether to fold or call or raise."

"And it's poker, not Tiddlywinks," added Smiert.

"Sometimes being captain is a game of — oh sod it, you get the picture."

"So what have you decided?" asked Jones.

"I'm going to fold."

Smiert coughed politely.

"Or raise. Whichever of those is the butch one." Daisy moved towards the rear exit.

"Wait," called Jones, "Where are you going?"

Daisy paused on the threshold of the door. "To beat the shit out of an eight-foot tall, slavering bastard, save my ship and everyone on New Amsterdam." She pulled at the door handle. The door remained shut. She pulled again, harder. And again. The door steadfastly refused to open.

Smiert coughed again.

"It's, it's actually locked," Jones rubbed the back

of his neck awkwardly, "You need to . . . flip the . . . the door lock, you need to . . ."

Daisy looked down and flipped the door lock open. "Right, I'll go and . . . right."

She left the room quickly before the others could spot the red flush now threatening to burn off her face.

KETTLEWICK HAD NOT EXPECTED that the captain would accept defeat so quickly.

Although he was not entirely surprised.

Given the time pressure and her desperate, pathetic need to save the people of New Amsterdam, her decision was the only sensible option available to her. Soon, he would have an entire crew at his disposal.

His chest balls throbbed with anticipation in their milk. *Soon, my pretties, soon.*

Two figures came clanking down the stairs from the operations room.

Jones and Smiert walked almost nonchalantly across the cargo bay and squared off against him.

The idiot XO casually tossed a ball up and down in one hand. The other hand gripped a baseball bat.

Smiert held a pair of taser devices, just like the one that bastard science officer had previously used on him. Oh yes, Tongue would suffer for that impertinence. A fatal Bible thrashing was too good for that one.

"XO. Doctor," Kettlewick greeted them, "What have we here?"

"We're the advance guard," said Jones. "Just waiting on security to arrive and then we're going to monster you up. Monster."

Kettlewick inclined his featureless black orb of a head. "Security are on holiday," he said. "They went on a stag 'all weekender' last year and they have yet to return."

"True," said Jones, slightly less cocky. "But you're forgetting one thing."

"Oh, and what, pray tell, is that, prey?"

"Humufell bling snandwank," mumbled Jones.

"Ah," said Kettlewick, "Yes, I must admit I had not considered that. Silly me. Now, amusing as your pathetic attempts to stall me are, my patience grows thin. Unlike these." Kettlewick raised a hand and extended his secondary talons.

"While I have to admit that under normal circumstances, the sight of those would make me foul my pants, these aren't normal circumstances. See,

I'm what you might call an armed prophet." Jones tossed the ball in the air, hefted the baseball bat, and swung.

For a split second, Kettlewick feared he had underestimated the XO. His fear was short-lived, however, as the ball struck him a glancing blow on the shoulder, bounced off, hit the PSG containers and fell to the floor, where it spun ineffectually for a bit before slowing and coming to a stop. There was a loud 'POP' sound as it burst open and discharged a puddle of thick orange gloop onto the floor. Not a ball then.

Kettlewick turned back to Jones and shrugged. "And that was supposed to do what, exactly?"

"Right," said Jones, glaring at the object. He gestured at it. "That was the other lucky grenade. I was sort of hoping it might blow you up again, like the first one."

"It might even have bruised him if you could hit straight," sneered the doctor.

"But if you *had* been successful, the grenade would have exploded, shattering the PSG containers and killing us all."

"Oh. Yeah," said Jones.

"That was lucky," said the doctor.

"Yes, it was," said Kettlewick. "But now your

luck has run out." He extruded his secondary talons once more and bent towards Jones. Dinner time.

A melodramatic voice rang out from the darkness. "Get away from him, you bitch!"

A mechanical stomping sound, 'clump, ptish, clump, ptish', followed the voice and Captain Daisy Daryl, once more awkwardly crammed into a cargo loader cage designed for giant seals, lumbered into the cargo bay.

She came to a halt before Kettlewick, twirling the exoskeleton's huge manipulator claws.

"Did you just call me a bitch?" asked Kettlewick.

Daisy nodded, "Yes. Well, it felt like it was going that way, so . . ."

"Huh'" said Kettlewick. "Well, we are full of surprises, Captain. But our jamboree bag has not yet been emptied of its contents."

"Our what?"

Kettlewick sighed. "Oh, never mind." He raised his arm.

Four grotesque figures emerged from behind the PSG containers and assembled themselves in a line behind Kettlewick.

"The Emergency Klaxons!" gasped Jones.

Smiert took a step forward, a look of awe and triumph on her face. "BlackWindow!" she breathed.

"No," Daisy said, "No, I think that one's Windy-Mane. Or was WindyMane. What have you done to them, Kettlewick?"

"Well, as I have explained to your science officer, I was somewhat at a loss to explain what these are for." Kettlewick raised the flap on his chest.

"Oh Jeebuzz, WHAT'S THAT?" screamed Jones.

The crew's faces twisted in disgust as he revealed the throbbing collection of white mozzarella-type balls nestling within his chest cavity.

"If I peel one of these away from myself and force it down the throat of an unsuspecting life form, it makes them undergo a forced mutation. They are not as beautiful as myself, of course; the skeletal ridges are a rather unpleasant grey and their distorted features are somewhat crude, but the overall effect is not unpleasant. Given time, they will grow into wonderful monstrosities. Nature truly is beautiful, is it not?" He replaced the flap. "Now, who wants to go first?"

Kettlewick had expected his little demonstration to elicit disgust, fear, perhaps some vomiting.

What he had not expected was to be grabbed by the throat and tossed unceremoniously across the room by Daisy's mechanical exoskeleton.

All hell broke loose around him.

#

With Kettlewick out of the way, Jones launched himself with a scream at the nearest Klaxon mutant. He was unsure if the scream was one of sheer terror or a newfound mix of bravery and battle lust, but he did not have time to think about it. If the creature had been as fast as it was disgusting, Jones would have been in trouble. But it was slow and ponderous, unused to its new physiology. Jones's baseball bat slammed hard into its misshapen head and bounced off without effect. Slow it may be, but it was also built like a tank.

The Klaxo-Morph looked blankly at him for a second, then reached out with a cybernetic arm.

"Oh, bollocks," said Jones.

He ducked as a something flew past his head, sparking and fizzing as it went — it was a disembodied cyber arm from one of the other Klaxo-Morphs. Well, at least someone was having better luck than he was. But the distraction had cost him precious seconds and his assailant took advantage of the lapse to grab him by the scruff of the neck and hurl him backwards. Jones hit the PSG drums and bounced off. He hit the deck hard. His jaws snapped shut, teeth jarring painfully together. Ouch. The Klaxo-Morph approached, nasty claw-like cyber things cyber-extruded from its cyber-arm. Jones watched, frozen in terror and morbid fascination, as certain death loomed. He was cyber-fucked.

The Klaxo-Morph was now only three steps away from him.

One step. Two.

As the creature took the third step, arm raised for the killing blow, a look of surprise crossed what now passed for its face. Arms wheeling comically, it slipped over backward and hit the deck. Triggered by the fall, a projectile weapon fired from its arm and tore into a cargo crane counterweight high above.

The restraining chain shattered, and the weight plummeted downward.

A wave of blood and entrails splashed over Jones.

"Aw, eeeeuw," Jones wiped at the mess.

Where a Klaxo-Morph had once been struggling to rise, there was now a pulped mess with a huge counterweight squatting on it.

Jones looked around and spotted what had caused the cyborg to slip. A boot-sized skid mark bisected the orange splodge that the lucky grenade had earlier expelled.

"Blimey," breathed Jones, "that was lucky."

#

Two Klaxo-Morphs advanced on Smiert, their cyber-arms held threateningly before them.

Judging by their slow, cumbersome movements, she could have outrun them, but she remained still.

They approached closer, closer.

Wait . . . wait . . . NOW!

Smiert brought the tasers to bear and pulled both triggers simultaneously.

The tiny hooks shot forward, embedding themselves in the chest units of the unsuspecting mutants.

Overcharged voltage surged through the wires, slamming into the mutated cyborgs. They halted their advance, jerking and shuddering as the electricity tore through them.

Then, as Smiert had calculated, their cybernetic units overloaded.

Arm, chest and leg implants, and one rather unfortunate eye implant, exploded in a shower of angry sparks. One cybernetic arm, its severed wires sparking and fizzing, flew away across the room.

The creatures collapsed to the floor, still

juddering and jerking, only now more from their exploding implants rather than voltage.

She smiled and nodded in satisfaction, dropping the now spent tasers.

Another figure emerged from the smoke.

A slow smile spread across Smiert's lips. "Hello *bambushkinski*," she said.

BlackWindow, morphed and twisted into a grotesque mix of zebroid and PSG monster, glared at her. "I really hate you," she slurred.

They say that luck is what happens when opportunity meets preparedness. When Kettlewick had escaped the airlock, the doctor had thought her plans ruined. How the hell was she going to get the bastard into her lab? But now here was Miss Golden Opportunity of the twenty-fourth century! She was perfect: part Ululation, part slavering monster. In the mutated BlackWindow, Smiert had everything she needed to produce an adult Starmane; a female Ululation with regenerative DNA.

Now all she had to do was to make sure that the object of her desire did not attain the object of *its* desire, which was, at this precise moment, to rip her head off.

"I'm going to eat your face," slurred Black-Window through what remained of her muzzle.

Shitski.

Smiert ducked as the mutant took a clumsy swipe at her. Recovering quickly, she bolted hard and fast for the nearest exit, BlackWindow in hot, lumbering pursuit.

Smiert felt no qualms about leaving her ship mates during battle: after all, by taking out two of the mutants, she had increased their odds of survival. The rest was up to them. Smiert had what she wanted and now her priority was to make sure it survived. For a while longer, at least.

She reached the main door and glanced over her shoulder to check BlackWindow's progress. Yes, there she was.

That's it, keep coming. You are furious. You hate me. I am so close now. Good horsey.

When BlackWindow was almost within arm's reach, Smiert slammed her hand onto the handprint pad.

Mercifully, the door slid open without delay. Smiert shot through, closely followed by an enraged BlackWindow.

The door slid shut and locked behind them.

KETTLEWICK, slightly dazed and very surprised, stood from where, a moment earlier, he had landed in a painful heap.

He had not expected the captain to react so fast. She appeared to have overcome her paralysing fear of him, which was irritating. He could feel another letter to the editor of *The Times* coming on. But that could wait. For now, he needed to —

A mechanical fist slammed into his armoured chest, propelling him backwards.

The blow was powerful, powerful enough to lift him off his feet and send him once more skidding across the cargo bay deck.

Thankfully, the punch had missed his chest balls.

His bulbous black head slammed into a stack of crates, and he lay dazed and winded.

The captain seemed to have discovered within herself a flair for violence. Who could have suspected? She would make an excellent Human-Morph. He growled to himself. Yes, he would give her the largest of his balls.

"I'm so sorry," blurted Daisy, "Are you alright? I really don't know how the seals control these bloody things."

Kettlewick revised his opinion of her downward.

Recovered from his battering, he stood, using the crates to lever himself upright.

"Perhaps, Captain, you should leave things you know little about to the experts. You are even worse at operating a cargo loader than you are at being a captain. Remarkable."

A mechanical fist shot out, smashing a hole in the crate behind him. Her punch was woefully wide of the mark.

"Oops, sorry. It's this neural interface you see. All I can think about is fish and then the loader gets all excited."

Another fist shot out, puncturing another hole in the crate on the other side of Kettlewick's head. He glanced impassively at the hole.

"You will note, I hope, my lack of fear. This should give you some sign of the awe in which I do not regard you."

"One last chance, Kettlewick," said Daisy. "This is a direct order from your captain. That's me, by the way. Stand down and let us help you. We can get you medical help or, if you prefer, we can drop you off on some uninhabited planet. Whatever you want. But get out of my way and let us deliver this cargo."

"I think not, 'Captain'." Kettlewick casually opened his chest flap. His chest balls quivered in milky anticipation. "Now, open wide."

Kettlewick slammed a fist into the centre of the cargo loader. It was too bulky and heavy for him to do any actual damage, of course. But his blow, combined with the cumbersome nature of the exoskeleton and its incompetent operator, had the desired effect.

The loader stumbled over its own clumping feet, tipped backwards, and crashed to the floor where it lay helpless, mechanical arms and legs flailing ineffectually.

"It was a bold attempt, Captain, but alas for nought."

A shout of fury erupted, closely followed by a

baseball bat-wielding Michigan Jones, who leapt onto the cargo loader. "Get back Kettlewick!"

"Mr Jones, really. That baseball bat will have no effect on me whatsoever."

Jones hesitated uncertainly. "Oh yeah? Well, what about this!" He whipped out a wire coat hanger. "Yeah? How d'you like them apples?"

"I detest apples. But not as much as I detest you."

"I warn you Kettlewick, I've sharpened this thing!"

"More than can be said for your wits, perhaps."

"Eh?"

"Quite." With a roar, Kettlewick swiped at the confused XO and swatted him aside.

Jones flew across the room, hit the bulkhead, and landed in an unconscious heap.

"Pathetic." Kettlewick shook his head. "Now then . . ."

He stood over the cargo loader.

What had been the captain's surprise weapon was now her prison. She stared up at Kettlewick, eyes wide. Kettlewick held out one of his dripping balls.

"Dear me," he said, "the admiral would be so disappointed."

"Well, that's just it," said Daisy, her tone surprisingly confident given the circumstances. "You see, I'm way past trying to impress anyone. Especially the admiral. His problem is he lets his wigs do his thinking for him."

"Wigs?"

"Yes. Smart wigs. He collects them. Lots of them. He's got a bunch in those crates behind you, as my XO recently reminded me. You know, those crates I just punched holes in. And see this?" she held up a hand. "Remote control."

She pressed a button.

Nothing happened.

"That's it? That's your big play? Dear me, you really are," Kettlewick said, leaning closer to her face, "a terrible captain."

"No," she replied, holding his glare. "I am a *terrifying* captain."

Smart wigs flew from the crate and swarmed over their target.

\#

Kettlewick flailed as three hundred and sixty-five wigs of various styles and colours covered his body, neural filaments extending, questing, piercing his exoskeleton, and integrating themselves with his nervous system.

His frantic movements came to a stop as his nervous system became slaved to the command of the wigs. Where before had stood an imposing eight-foot tall, terrifying mutant, there now stood a monster shaped mountain of hairy mats.

Daisy released a pent up breath. So far, so good.

"Proceed to power junction A7," Daisy said into the remote control. With multiple smart wigs now compelling him, Daisy knew, hoped, that Kettlewick would have no option but to obey. Trying and failing to resist their commands, he jerked towards the electrical power junction.

Come on, hurry up, hurry up!

She did not know how long the influence of the wigs would last. They were designed for humans, after all. She had to act fast before Kettlewick threw off control.

"Open junction box," she said.

With stiff, jerking movements, Kettlewick threw open the box.

"Extrude those secondary talons you're so fond of and pierce the main power cord."

"Bitch! I'll make you swallow all my balls!" he

screamed. He held his quivering talons just millime-
tres from the thick cable.

"Oh, shut up, Kettlewick," said Daisy. "Now
pierce the cable!"

Finally succumbing to the combined insistence
of multiple smart wigs, Kettlewick thrust his talons
into the power cable and, with a last scream of frustration and with thousands of volts of electrical
current coursing through him, promptly exploded.

STARTLED CREW PARTED to let her through as Smiert ran hard for her laboratory. But not too fast. She needed to stay in sight of BlackWindow in case she lost interest and vented her anger on some other unlucky crew member. Unlikely, she supposed, but she wasn't about to lose her prize now.

She rounded a corner and came skidding to a halt outside her lab.

A few heartbeats later, BlackWindow also rounded the corner where she stopped, a wicked snarl on her muzzle. She drew herself up and reached out, but before her claw could reach Smiert's face, the bulkhead door slammed shut, trapping her arm.

Tongue entered the corridor at a run from the other direction.

"You fool, what have you done?" Smiert spat.

Tongue glanced at the twitching arm.

"Saved you from that thing. Whatever it is," said Tongue. "Thank me later."

"Did you release the Jelloids? "

"Yes, but I still don't understand why. Those things are disgusting by the way."

Smiert bit her lip. "Did any of them mention cocktails?"

"What? No."

"Good, good. Now stand back," said Smiert, punching at the bulkhead release button.

She did not wait to see if Tongue had followed her instruction. She would have been happy for BlackWindow to tear the smug bastard apart.

Win-win.

Suddenly released, BlackWindow stumbled past the door and paused, relishing the impending kill.

She leapt for Smiert.

Smiert punched the open mechanism for the lab door.

The doctor felt the wind rush out of her as Black-Window slammed her hard against the bulkhead. With one claw pinning her in place, BlackWindow drew back her other fist and extended her secondary talons.

Smiert almost laughed as a thick, fleshy tentacle wrapped itself around BlackWindow's neck.

Surprised, the Ululation-morph looked around and found herself staring into the fleshy maw of a huge Spongiform Jelloid Lifeform. Forced to release Smiert, she braced and crouched low, resisting the brute strength of the Jelloid, which was now trying to pull her through the door and into the lab.

For a moment, there was a stalemate, as each of the combatants resisted the power and strength of the other. But more tentacles whipped out, wrapping themselves around BlackWindow's limbs.

Millimetre by millimetre, the mutant lost ground.

Now at the threshold of the laboratory door, she raised her legs, placing her feet midway up the wall on either side of the door frame, bracing herself against the Jelloid's strength.

Again there was stalemate.

BlackWindow released her grip on one tentacle and extended the barrel of her hoof-gun. With a snarl of defiance, she rapid-fired volley after volley of bullets point-blank into the Jelloid's maw.

In response, thick, powerful tentacles lashed out and ensnared her shooting arm, yanking it viciously up and to the side. Bullets tore uselessly into the ceiling as more and more tentacles reached out and wrapped around the struggling Ululation-Morph until they enveloped her.

With a final inhuman scream the Jelloid pulled her into the lab.

Smiert punched the door control, and it slammed shut. She hit the lock.

"YES! That was why," Smiert panted, enjoying the look of horror on the Yerbootsian's face.

"OK, I understand the why, but . . . why?"

"Ululation DNA combined with Kettlewick's regenerative properties. My Jelloids are very, *very* good at deconstructing DNA code. With this and original Starmane's mane hair, I have complete blueprint. I can now speed-grow Ululation egg fertilised with the coming of the herald of the second coming."

"Fertilised with the — oh, I see. And I really wish I didn't. So all we need now is Jones's . . . coming."

Smiert held up a sample tube.

"What is — oh Jeebuzz, how the hell did you get that?"

"Easy," said Smiert. "There is ocean of the stuff in computer core. In small quantities the PSG is *very* effective aphrodisiac."

Tongue pulled a face. "You enjoy your work way

too much, you know that, don't you? Now, where's the captain?"

Smiert was lost in thought, admiring the fluid in the sample tube. "Who?" she said absently.

"STATUS, MR POWER?" said Daisy as she and Jones strolled onto the bridge.

"Oh, er, Captain, welcome back. We'll be arriving at New Amsterdam in about fifteen minutes, all ship's functions normal, which is to say on the verge of total collapse. The computer has been nice and quiet since the reboot. Oh, I'm now a god by the way."

Jones turned to Daisy. "Fifteen minutes. That's cutting it fine."

"I fought a black hole made of limerent gravity."

"Yes," said Daisy. "I hope they can offload it in time."

"And I can channel the power of the big bang. There's this word you see and —"

"Is this an official report, Mr Power?" said Daisy.

"Er, well no, you see I —"

"Well, I look forward to reading all about it. Officially. In your official report. Later."

Steve deflated. "Right, fine, whatever. I'll just man the helm, shall I?"

Jones grinned. "Still, your dad won't be very pleased at the delay."

"Correct Mr Jones, I am very much displeased!" boomed the admiral's voice. His angry face filled the main viewscreen. "What the hell is going on? The New Amsterdam government is going ballistic!"

"Incoming transmission, Captain," said Mic Vol from the communications station.

"Yes, thank you Mr Vol, I had noticed," said Daisy dryly.

"Er, sorry Captain," said Steve, "Mic's got a bit of a temporal displacement thing going on."

"I am waiting for an explanation, Daisy," demanded the admiral.

"Steve, why does he look red? What's wrong with the colour balance?" asked Jones.

"Nothing, all normal."

"I think that's his actual face colour," said Daisy.

"Well?"

"Well, Admiral, we had a bit of an accident with the 1960s Purple Sex Gas, which turned our chief engineer into an eight-foot tall, slavering psychopath, had to reboot the computer to remove his override-override, and then swing around a black hole to get us back on schedule. I think that's everything?" Daisy raised a questioning eyebrow at Jones.

"Oh, and then I saved us all by using my face tat —"

"XO? That was everything?"

"Well, there was the thing where me and you . . ." Jones held up his hands, making a crude gesture.

"Yes, that was everything," said Daisy, primly. "We'll be arriving at New Amsterdam in just under fifteen minutes."

"Well, it's damn lucky for you they have those cargo transporter beam things, otherwise the whole batch would have been useless. I am not pleased by this at all, young lady. You have put this mission in danger of failure, risking millions of lives. Not to mention my invoice. Michigan Jones, I hereby promote you to the rank of captain. Daisy, you are dismissed."

"No," said Daisy.

"I beg your pardon?"

"Beg all you like, Dad, it won't make any difference. This is my ship; I am the captain. Captain Daisy Daryl. Daisy 2.0 if you like. Hello. Besides,

Mr Jones has no desire to take command — do you?" Daisy said, her voice dripping with not-so-veiled hints of violence.

"No thanks. I've seen what you can do to huge death mutants with chest balls and I don't want any of that in my face."

"Daisy," the admiral railed from the viewscreen, "you're not impressing anyone you know!"

"No, I'm not," she said, "that's rather the point. Viewscreen off."

"How dare you! I —"

Mic cut off the admiral mid-vent.

"Lens flare, Mr Jones," said Daisy. "We should get some lens flare on the bridge. And we need an exposition officer."

"A what?"

"Never mind. Now, I don't know about you, but I could do with a shower before we arrive at New Amsterdam."

"Excellent idea, Captain. Steve, you have the conn."

Captain Daisy Daryl and her XO Michigan Jones walked off the bridge.

As the bridge door squealed shut behind them, Jones halted. He took a small canister from his pocket.

"What's that?" asked Daisy.

He showed her. "I . . . just wondered . . ." he said.

She smiled. "Excellent suggestion XO. Um, how would you feel about wearing a uniform shirt open from here to here?" She drew her hand down from her neck to her belt. "And oil? Ever thought about oiling up while on duty?"

Jones smiled. "Well, we could always try a proof of concept?"

As they continued along the corridor, Jones slipped the canister of 1960s purple sex gas back into his pocket.

D EEP WITHIN HYPOSPACE , two elemental figures sat in the centre of a vast, empty ballroom decorated in baroque opulence. One figure was an enormous boulder, the other a curled filament.

They regarded one another across a gaming table.

Neither of them knew why they were in this particular place; both supposed it to be something to do with some long-forgotten arcane rule of the space in which they existed.

The black and white chequered pattern of the floor mimicked the chequered pattern of their playing board. On the table next to the board rested a large, dusty tome and a quill.

Any creature not native to this realm would perceive the garish surroundings to be slightly . . . 'off', as if the two players were projected against a photograph of a ballroom rather than actually being there. But then any creature not native to hypospace would go instantly insane and eat its own face, so the oddness of the surroundings would be the least of its worries.

"So," said Boulder.

"So," agreed Filament.

"Round two to me, I think."

"Hmm. I could not see your purpose with the gas until it was too late. Then it was a matter of keeping my own pieces alive. You forced me to play a defensive game."

"Indeed. You are no further forward, whereas my strategies are much advanced."

Filament chuckled at that.

"You disagree?" demanded Boulder.

"No, I don't."

"Yes you do."

"No, I really don't."

"You're doing it now."

"So I am," said Filament, chuckling once more.

"Ah, then you agree you disagree?"

"Perhaps we should agree to disagree on the point of whether I agree we disagree. Agreed?"

"No . . . I think," said Boulder.

"Well, let me put it this way. You disagree that we should agree to disagree on the point of whether or not I agree we disagree, whereas we can agree that we agree on the point of my agreement with your statement that I disagree and yet were I to agree that we disagree on your first point, then in fact we would agree that we agree based on the agreement that I agree we disagree. Agreed?"

"Let me put it this way," Boulder carefully considered his argument for a moment, "Sod off. Yes, I think that nicely sums up my position."

"So you disagree?"

Boulder leaned forward, or that is to say, it rolled itself slightly towards Filament. "You. Lost." Satisfied, it rolled back again. Point made, it inspected a piece on the gaming board. "Do you really think they are alive?"

Filament regarded him for a moment. "In a sense."

"In what sense?"

"In the sense that some pieces are alive whilst others are not dead."

"You really are a sore loser, aren't you?"

"I am quite sore. I think it's this chair. There's not much padding. And it's certainly not designed for entities incorporating as filaments. Why are we in this place, anyway?"

"I make that one draw, and one clear win. For me," Boulder was determined not to let Filament distract from the brilliance of its victory.

"Some fresh air I think." Filament stretched itself to its full length, extending beyond and through the cavernous ceiling of the ballroom with its paintings of fleshy angels and awestruck humans. It extended itself far above the fairy-tale castle which housed them and looked around. The castle stood like a shout of architectural triumph atop a broad hill. Above it, a billion stars twinkled in the night sky.

"Do you mind?" said the Castle.

"Oh sorry, beg pardon."

Filament released its stretch, retracting to its usual curled state, once more facing its opponent across the gaming board.

"Happy now?" asked Boulder.

"It is possible to win the battle yet still lose the war."

"Tell that to the person who . . . won the battle and the war."

"You don't think there's the slightest possibility I may have won the game before we even started?"

Boulder considered for a moment. "No," it said. "For a start, that would be cheating. Like a runner who's off the blocks before they have fired the starting pistol."

"Ah, but what if all the runners were shot dead with the starting pistol? In that case, there could be no cheating since the race ended before it started."

"And no winners."

"Except the person with the pistol."

À propos of nothing, a humanoid lion incorporated next to them. It blinked a few times as if surprised to be there and then danced to a jaunty song, its padded feet slap-slapping on the cold tiles of the floor.

"Yes, thank you, not now," Boulder dismissed the lion with a wave of its hand. Or whatever the analogue of a boulder's hand might be.

The entity known within hypospace as 'Kris the Sleeveless Lion and his Singing Trousers' stopped dancing. He looked a bit hurt for a moment, then shrugged and dis-incorporated.

Filament sighed. "I really do not understand this place."

"I'm hungry. Is this table edible, do you think?"

"No."

"Then why's it called a dining table?"

"It isn't. It's a gaming table. Oh." Filament picked up the book and quill and began writing.

"What are you doing?"

"My new hobby. I am compiling a Dictionary of the Undefined."

"Oh," said Boulder, not sure what that meant.

"Expresso," said Filament, scribbling into the book.

"You mean Espresso. That's not undefined."

"No, 'Expresso'. Which is hereby defined as 'the communication of ideas through the expression of milk'."

"How is it undefined if you've defined it?"

"That's the point, my dear Boulder. I give them a definition. You can't just let new words and phrases go around undefined. They appear randomly out of the quantum foam of the collective unconscious, and if not quickly defined, they can attach themselves to all sorts of nasty concepts. Like 'Man Paste'."

"What's man paste?"

"I've no idea. But unless it gets recorded and defined, it could mean any kind of unpleasantness. How would you know what is meant by the phrase 'he went around the hospital spreading his man paste'?"

"I wouldn't. And it sounds disgusting."

"Exactly. Left to its own devices, it would attach itself to concepts that would be better left undefined. Therefore, I shall give it a more palatable definition. In this case," Filament considered for a moment, "Yes, I shall define 'man paste' to mean 'succour'."

"That still sounds disgusting."

"Indeed — a prime example. Had the word 'succour' remained undefined, it would most likely have self-defined as meaning 'to suck one's own' —"

"Yes, shut up now."

"Bollocks."

"Excuse me?"

"Another example. 'Bollocks' wasn't caught in time and it went feral. Attracted all sorts of silliness; there's plain old 'bollocks', which can mean either total nonsense or a crude reference to male genitalia, which is bad unless the genitalia in question belong to a dog, because 'the dog's bollocks' are generally considered as being a good thing; there's 'bollocksed up', which is a disastrously bad thing; 'drop a bollock' which is quite embarrassing and usually results in 'a bollocking' —"

"Yes, yes, I take your point. So, shall we begin round three?"

"Very well," Filament put down his quill. "But I feel you will regret your eagerness. Or, as my dictionary would have it, you will soon be in an engorged state of 'foamy quiff'."

Boulder sighed and moved a piece on the board. "Your move."

<<<<>>>>

THE END

THE KETTLEWICK MONSTER IS DEAD

*BUT THE CREW OF SPACE SCRAP 17 SHALL
RETURN IN*

'THE BISCUITS OF WAR'

ACKNOWLEDGEMENTS

As usual massive thanks to Samantha for putting up with my frowning into the distance, mumbling, gnashing teeth, growling and drinking all the coffee. And for introducing me to the word 'limerent'. I'm hoping she didn't need to learn it as a means of describing me. Thanks to Suzanne and editors Anya and Mark for risking their sanity trying to make sense of my word salad (oh, now there's an idea for a YouTube channel...). And thanks to Debesh, for his unwavering support and making sure I don't trip over my own mistakes.

You're all spiffing.

ALSO BY ERICK DRAKE

Space Scrap 17

Book 1: *The Doomsday Machine*

Book 2: *1960s Purple Sex Gas*

Book 3: *The Biscuits of War*

Short Stories

Elashom The Great Refuses And Other Stories

For more information about Erick Drake content and books visit

www.erickdrake.com

Independent author Erick Drake is a writer of 'weird' fiction; sci-fi, dark fantasy, alternative history and comedy (which ranges from the absurd to the dark, depending on his mood). More details may be found on his website www.erickdrake.com.

He has written sketches for BBC radio comedy and in 2004 was commissioned by BBC South to write a Doctor Who TV story ('The Paradox Device' – production was cancelled due to some upstart genius called Russell T. Davies rebooting the series).

Currently living in Essex with his wife and cat, Erick is surrounded by the rich landscapes of the Essex countryside.

facebook.com/erickdrake616

twitter.com/@SpaceScrap17

instagram.com/erickdrake616

Until next time . . .